WALK AWAY &
FORGET HIM

Walk Away and Forget Him is an incredibly moving, funny and truthful insight into what life can really be like for a large percentage of our population. Gerry's honesty as he brings us through his journey is a superb performance from a first-time author. The bond he had with his mother is incredibly touching to read and should inspire all us reserved Irish men to publicly proclaim how we feel about 'the Mammy', without any fear!

I vividly remember Nellie Maguire powerfully wheeling her son Gerard as a child through Ballyfermot. I always suspected she was a very different, dignified and powerful mother – now I know it's true.

A stunning and memorable read that I would recommend to everyone.

Joe Duffy, RTÉ

Walk Away & Forget Him

Gerry Maguire

MERLIN
PUBLISHING

First published in 2009 by
Merlin Publishing
Newmarket Hall, Cork Street,
Dublin 8, Ireland
Tel: +353 1 4535866
Fax: +353 1 4535930
publishing@merlin.ie
www.merlinwolfhound.com

ISBN 978-1-903582-89-3

A CIP catalogue record for this book is available from the
British Library.

10 9 8 7 6 5 4 3 2 1

Typeset by Gough Typesetting Services, Dublin
Cover Design by Graham Thew Design
Cover image courtesy of www.istockphotos.com © Michael Fernahl
Printed and bound by CPI Cox & Wyman, Britain

DEDICATION

My main reason for writing the book is to let the world know what I have always known and that is just how awe-inspiringly wonderful my mother was. Barely an hour goes by when I don't think just how desperately I miss her and how lost and sad I am without her. She truly was the light of my life. I know, without her ever telling me, as I never needed her to, that she was so proud of me. I hope that if she was still here, and read the book, that her pride would not be diminished as it would break my heart if it was.

I know that when I meet her again in the great beyond that she'll say to me: "You big eejit for saying those things about me!"

She may be right.

But they are straight from this big eejit's heart!

ACKNOWLEDGEMENTS

Whenever anyone prepares to thank people for what they may have done for them over a particular period of time, they will always preface their remarks by apologising to those to whom thanks should be given but were not due to a genuine error of omission. This is all the more likely to happen when you look back to a life stretching back to 1962, as I do in this book. So to those whom I have left out, I am sorry.

Firstly, I would like to thank my publishers, Merlin, and in particular my editor Aoife, and Chenile and Julie. You have shown more faith in me than I have in myself and for that I am so grateful. Our journey of telling my story is now completed and I thank you for sticking with me. Thanks also to Sonya from O'Neill Quinn Limited for all your advice during this journey.

I know it's always dangerous to single out one person for particular attention, but I would never forgive myself if I let this opportunity pass without particularly mentioning my orthotist, Kieran Hurley. Many will not know what an orthotist is or have even heard the word before. In short, an orthotist makes artificial devices to enable those who require them to walk. I have required the use of callipers to allow me to walk for all of my life and for more than 30 years, Kieran has been my orthotist.

He has made and repaired my callipers for all those years. I have entrusted my very safety with him and in times of trouble he has never let me down. Due to the constant wear and tear which they are exposed to, callipers always seem to breakdown at the most inopportune times and I have, therefore, had to call on Kieran's help at some most unsociable hours. He has never once failed me and has gotten me mobile again in double quick time. He has been a true friend and I am so pleased to be able to publicly acknowledge the vital role which he and his God-given talents have played in my life.

To all the many friends, past and present, which I have made in the last three decades in the Department of Health. I could write a book on my experiences there if only I hadn't signed the Official Secrets Act!

I've been blessed to have the family and extended family that I have. To Dominic, Anne and Liam – I'm an Irish man so I'm never going to say the following to your faces! I love the three of you so much and am so incredibly proud to be your brother. I can't thank you enough for the many times when the three of you have been there for me over the years and you should be under no illusions as to the massive part which the three of you have played, individually and collectively, in helping me get to this day.

And finally to the two people who brought me into this world, Nellie and Willie Maguire, my Ma and Da. I'd be lying if I didn't say that there have been times when I wished you hadn't. Hopefully this book will clarify those thoughts. But be assured that even when those thoughts invaded my psyche, my love for the two of you never dimmed.

My father used cycle to work. In his last job he worked shift work – 7am-3pm and 3pm-11pm. One day, when he was on the early shift, I was in the front garden washing my car. It was around 3.30 when I looked up and there he was cycling down the middle of the road. "Howya Ger," he said as he dismounted. I said: "You looked like John Wayne riding down the centre of the town on his way to save it from the baddies!" For, in essence, that's what he was to me – the hero, my hero. The one I longed to be like but fell so far short of.

And then there's my Ma – the reason for my writing this book. I wanted the world to know what I always knew and that was that I knew the greatest woman who ever lived. She'd be furious with me for talking about her in such terms as she was such an unassuming, intensely self-deprecating person. Until I breathe my last breath, I will never stop missing her. In the 1960s and '70s, many sitting room mantelpieces in Ireland were adorned by china plates, varying in size, dedicated to the mother of the house. The verse on the plates, though corny, still lives in my memory and with thanks to the unknown author, I re-visit it now:

> 'To one who bears the sweetest name
> And adds a lustre to the same
> Who shares my joys, who cheers when sad
> The greatest friend I ever had
> Long life to her for there's no other
> Can take the place of my dear mother.'

CONTENTS

ONE

AGAINST THE ODDS

I remember reading a newspaper article when I was young which said that there was a higher risk of a child being born with a handicap when the expectant mother was approaching 40 years or over. I was annoyed with my mother when I did the maths in my head and realised that she was in her fortieth year when she gave birth to me. I never had the nerve to ask her why she had me so late, in case I got a clip around the ear! Instead I thought, 'If only she hadn't gotten pregnant'. Of course that would have meant that I would never have been born...

Spina Bifida are two words which fill prospective parents with such fear and dread. On the scale of potential abnormalities with your unborn child, it is right up there with the worst. In the 1960s, tests to detect potential problems with the unborn child during pregnancy were unheard of. The inevitable result was that preparing psychologically to bring a child with a disability into the world was not a luxury afforded to any parents – including mine.

Spina Bifida is a condition which comes under the heading of a Neural Tube Defect. This means basically that if you take the neural tube as being the main line connecting the brain and the spine, then you really don't want to have a defect there. One of the most visible signs of this in newborns is a bulge or a hole at the base of the spine. This is where the spine has not fused into one long, life-giving mainline to the brain. There are two inevitable results: either the spine is not strong enough to allow the person to walk without artificial help in their lives and/or the brain is pummelled by pressure, resulting in an accumulation of fluid which needs constant draining. This is done through a shunt which can have a cumulative negative effect on the kidneys and bladder. The build up of fluid, Hydrocephalus, results in the newborn's head size being significantly larger than other babies' heads. It's a trait which will last throughout the person's life.

On the morning of August 31, 1962, my parents, probably more accurately my mother, were faced with such a crushing blow. My Ma had already given birth to three healthy children, Dominic aged 7, Anne, 6, and Liam, 4, within a four year period. I was the last of her family and was arriving after a four and a half year gap. And so it was that in the maternity unit of what was then St Kevin's Hospital, Dublin, now St James's, that my mother brought me into her changed, and changed utterly, world.

Surgery to try to close or fuse the spine is inevitable. The surgery is so extensive that it results in fairly obvious scar damage which remains for the rest of your life. I had this surgery fairly soon after birth and carry such a badge of honour to this day. However the surgery is only remedial. It does not, nor can it, result in the spine functioning normally. Sadly, once the condition has invaded the child's body in the womb there is no turning back.

All in all it ain't no bowl of cherries for the mother to be or for the poor little sod whose life of struggle is about to begin.

It took some time for the medics to confirm for my parents that baby Gerard was one of the unlucky ones. There was good news though. They were told: "Your baby does not have Hydrocephalus. He will, however, never walk. My advice to you is to put him in a home and forget about him. You have three other healthy children, go and enjoy them."

Such was the medical advice given to my parents in the weeks after my birth. I remember some fifteen years later my mother pointing out to me the doctor who had told them this. We were in the National Rehabilitation Hospital in Dun Laoghaire at the time. I said we should go over and remind him what he had said all those years before. But such was the dignity of the woman, that my mother saw no point in being triumphalist by showing this doctor that his doomsday prognosis had turned out to be so wrong. In her eyes the proof of his misinformation, rather than his misdiagnosis, was in the beloved son sitting beside her, waiting for yet another hospital outpatient appointment to come around. She needed no validation of the choice she had made when she decided to ignore that doctor's advice.

I was told later that the first few weeks were touch and

go for the newest Maguire but nobody ever went into that much detail. Those first weeks were in the days before easy access to the telephone so the methods of communicating any of the problems I was having in hospital to my family, a little over five miles away, were difficult. My father found this to be the case a couple of weeks after I was born when the Gardaí called to our house early one morning. They told him to get to the hospital as quickly as possible, as it was felt that I could die at any minute. My mother was with me as she waited to see if God was about to make the decision on my future.

I remember my father telling me how scared he was when he saw me, looking so small in this huge oxygen tent, struggling for life. My parents were told to prepare for the worse as it was unlikely that I was going to get through this. My mother, convinced, neither for the first time or the last time in the power of prayer, was completely unwilling to let me go and her prayers were answered. I did pull through but this was just the harbinger of the many battles to come.

This was apparently only one of a few times when I came close to dying as a baby. It became a nightly routine for Dominic, Anne and Liam to be gathered around our sitting room by my father to say the Rosary with my recovery as its intention, while my mother kept a bedside vigil at the hospital. Looking back, it must have been slightly surreal for them praying for a brother whom they had rarely seen. They could probably scarcely remember me since so much of my life since birth had been spent in hospital.

There were times when my mother was advised just to let things take their course and to allow me to slip away.

Again this advice was accompanied by the medical belief that this would not only be best for me but also for her. The feeling was that it would save her from many years of struggle, were I to survive. But from stories I have heard, mainly from my aunts in whom she would have confided, my mother was adamant that they should do everything physically, surgically and medically possible to keep me alive. Looking back, I never had the experience of my mother telling me about what I'm sure were incredible dilemmas for her to cope with. The fact that she didn't ever share those experiences with me in later life only convinces me all the more of just how traumatic those times must have been for her. From what my aunts tell me, she never once gave them the impression that the thought of taking the option of letting me go ever entered her head. And knowing how unsentimental and clear thinking she was about what was right and what was wrong, I don't think that she ever wanted me to know it was even suggested. She would have hated the idea that she might potentially devalue my existence in any way by acknowledging that such propositions were put to her at the time.

The determination of my mother, Ellen (Nellie to those who knew her), was evident from day one of my life. A devout Catholic, brought up in Connolly Gardens in the posh part (as my father used say!) of Inchicore in West Dublin, she believed fervently that everything happened as part of God's plans. As a child and young adult she was very active in the Church, with various things from prayer groups to the Legion of Mary. Her faith, therefore, was not only a part of her but she was also proud to profess it. So to abdicate her responsibility of caring for her child, regardless of what disability he had, or what difficulties that disability was inevitably going to bring, would have been such a dereliction of her faith that I don't believe that she would, or indeed did, consider it for a second. Once I got a bit stronger she convinced the medics, against all their combined advice, that she would see that I would walk and be as independent as possible. After that was accepted the initial plan of action was very simple. I would require daily physiotherapy, regular surgical procedures and in-patient review at the Richmond Hospital, which is now, sadly, no longer in existence.

The young family Maguire had only a few months previously moved from my father, Willie's, family home on Anner Road, Inchicore, to the new and potentially bustling housing estate in Ballyfermot. It was a big move as Ballyfermot was almost considered to be in the country! Willie and Nellie and the kids had settled in happily there just before I was born. A few years later I used to make them laugh when the TV series "The Little House on the Prairie" aired in the early 1970s. The two spoilt brats in the town were called Nellie and Willie and here we were with parents of the same names! I think it was the juxtaposition of the characters in the programme against my parents' characters which got them going. You really would struggle to meet two less spoiled individuals in life than Willie and Nellie Maguire.

Public transport from Ballyfermot to the Richmond Hospital, on the north side of the River Liffey, was neither convenient nor reliable. But start out on this treatment plan my mother did, always with the unshakable belief that God would grant her what she wanted. For much of my early days, parenting of Dominic, Anne and Liam, was done by my mother during the day, while my Da was at work. My father then took over at night, while my Ma was with me in the hospital. They literally must have been like ships passing in the night. They must have been worn out on many occasions with my Ma caring for three young children and also attending to a baby in hospital and my father working as a labourer in a building company – damned hard work for damned little money – and then taking over from my Ma when he got home from work as she headed off to the hospital.

My earliest memories all centre firmly around my mother, hardly surprising given the initial three year journey we were undertaking. Despite the intensive physiotherapy and surgical interventions, it became clear that my spine was irreparably damaged. It was too inadequate to enable me to walk unaided. The medics advised my mother that I would, maybe, be able to eventually walk a few steps with the aid of metal callipers on both legs. They told her that she should prepare herself for some tough times while I got used to the callipers, as they would cause me a lot of pain and discomfort which both of us would find distressing. And from what I can remember they weren't wrong!

The process of getting used to callipers and the basic task of just putting them on, began soon afterwards. My little frame had being preparing for the heavy, metal callipers over those first few years in the Richmond, left leg calliper up to my thigh, right leg one to my knee. Other boys of my age would simply learn how to stick on their socks and shoes and they were up and about. For me then, as it still is now, it was a matter of starting slowly every day by putting my left leg calliper on first. It's attached to surgical boots, with a strap closing at my calf. There's a leather knee-pad which became, de-facto, my knee-cap and attached around my knee and then there were closing straps at my thigh. Then it would be the turn of the right leg calliper. Again it's attached by spurs leading to a surgical boot. As the right leg calliper was knee-length, the straps closed at the knee. From as far back as I can remember, Mammy always insisted that I put these on myself, such was her determination that I become as independent and self-sufficient as quickly as possible. She watched closely and taught me how to do it until I was fully familiar with the drill. Whilst it was tortuously time-consuming as a child, now I've gotten it down to a three minutes maximum job!

One of the real pains I remember as a child were the surgical boots provided by the State. As my left leg was some inches shorter than my right, the boots were built up with a lift on the heel and sole which made them look cosmetically disgusting. It also made them ripe for other kids to point at, and of course to look at me. They'd ask their parents, never in a very subtle way, why I had to wear this big shoe. Needless to say, my self-esteem was already taking a bit of a battering. To make matters worse, the State provided only one pair at a time. We couldn't replace them until the boots could be proven to be beyond hope of any potential repair. It was the same with the callipers.

One of my earliest memories is when I was about four or five years old, at most, and I am trying to walk for the first time with the aid of these heavy, metal callipers. My Auntie Maureen tells a story of how she used to try to encourage me to walk but I would regularly fall over. My Mother would never let her pick me up, insisting that I pick myself up. And she was right to be like that. It would have been so easy for her to cosset and over-protect me. But she was seeing the bigger picture – the long road which lay ahead of me. I'm sure it broke her heart to see me struggling to my feet when I fell but her approach was exactly the right one.

My first successful solo walk is etched on my brain. Talk about one small step for man. This was indeed one giant leap for the young Gerard! I remember it was a really sunny day as my mother knelt at the window in our sitting room. I was standing precariously maybe five or six feet away from her. I'm sure I had many falls before I successfully made that short journey into her arms without falling but eventually I did complete it. What I remember so vividly, as if the very event had only happened yesterday, was my mother crying as I half-fell, half-launched myself into her out-stretched arms. The next time I saw her cry was nearly 20 years later when my father died. Those tears on that sunny day in the mid-1960s in our living room, shared by just her and me, were tears, I'm sure, of joy but also of vindication, of a feeling of *"I knew we could do it!"*

After mastering (ok, mastering may be gilding the lily just a bit!) this, my Ma said that the one time that I was always guaranteed to get to my feet quickly was when the song 'The Huckelbuck' sung by Brendan Bowyer came on the radio. I'd get to my feet and try to dance to it but didn't do it very successfully. I'd get to the "Huckle" bit but more often than not would have fallen when it came to the "Buck"!

So many neighbours I've spoken to since have recounted seeing my mother and me leaving early every morning on our journey to the Richmond. Given how

pessimistic the medics were about me ever walking,
Mammy felt that for a long while they approached my
treatment as going through the motions, waiting until
she would eventually give up. They reckoned, however,
without her indomitable spirit. She had a conviction that
I would walk, not in any proving people wrong way, for
that was not her style, but in an unswerving commitment
to doing the very best for one of her own, and by God did
she succeed in that.

Following my completed physio treatment at the
Richmond, my medical care was transferred to Our Lady's
Hospital for Sick Children in Crumlin. I must have broken
Mammy's heart so many times as I had to have so many
operations which she helped prepare me for but which I
begged and begged her to prevent happening. As a young
child, I was so terrified of having to go into hospital. I
dreaded waiting on the morning of operations for this
stranger, who I now know was with the Anaesthetics
staff, to arrive, give me an injection in the backside, which
stung like hell, and then be wheeled down to the operating
theatre. My memories of that horrible smell of ether and
the other forms of anaesthesia they used are still vivid
today, over 40 years later. Is it any wonder that I was scared
silly not only facing this at such a young age, but facing it
without my mother at my side. She used to have to wait
patiently at home until she was allowed to come in and
see me at visiting time. Given the fact that she wouldn't
even have had access to a telephone so that she could
ring to see how the operations were progressing, she must
have been so scared on the bus journey to the hospital,
not knowing what news or sight was awaiting her. How
unbearably difficult it must have been for her, denied even

the consolation of staying on the hospital premises, but such a rigid approach to hospital care existed then. Parents today are so rightly allowed, and encouraged, to take an active part in their sick child's treatment in hospital. It can help them to cope with what is happening and to make sure that their child doesn't feel so isolated at such a vulnerable time. Looking back both Mammy and myself were as lonely and as scared as each other, I'm sure.

These were feelings that we both had to get used to as so many more operations followed, so many lonely days and nights spent in St Joseph's ward in Our Lady's. The amount of times I spent on that ward, in that hospital, both as an inpatient and an outpatient, being treated by doctors Brady and Regan! I remember so many times seeing my mother talking to them and wondering what they were talking about and yet being too afraid to ask my mother for fear that I would hear something which I didn't want to know. I vividly remember the awful fear which I felt when my Ma would bring me to the hospital for an outpatient visit as this would invariably lead to a longer stay. I knew then, as I know now, exactly why I hated going into hospital: firstly, there was the intense loneliness which I was going to feel and secondly, and much more acutely, being separated from my adored mother.

Even at that young age, I remember wondering to myself just why I was having so many operations which didn't seem to be making me any better. And then the horrible thought struck me that maybe Mammy was putting me into hospital so that she might get a rest from me. I was terrified to ask her for fear that this, in fact, was the truth. Looking back, I realise that what I was thinking was so incredibly far from the truth. Mammy was, as she always did, just trying to improve my quality of life, even if it meant her leaving me in a place which I'm sure that she, broken-heartedly, knew that I hated.

Visiting times in Our Lady's were strict, rigidly strict. One hour in the afternoon, one hour in the evening. My mother came to see me every evening, without fail, taking the 78 bus from Ballyfermot to Kilmainham and the 23 bus from Kilmainham to Crumlin. Doing the journey now with improved and more available public transport and cars at everyone's beck and call, would be fine. In the late 1960s and early '70s it must have been a nightmare for her. Bus strikes were also such a regular occurrence then. To try to help make ends meet, my mother by this stage had gotten a job in the Dominican Convent in Ballyfermot. Given the fact that some of my stays in hospital would drag on for weeks, allied to taking care of her three other children and working during the day in the laundry and kitchen in the convent, my mother was an incredible woman. I'm not sure how she managed to juggle everything. Sometimes, during my periods out of hospital, she used to bring me to work if there was nobody available to look after me and I witnessed at first hand just how hard she worked. When you consider that she did all of this and ran her family home, her efforts were nothing short of superhuman.

My days pre- and post-surgery in hospital centred on waiting for evening time and that precious one hour visiting time when she would arrive. I used to sit patiently (no pun intended) waiting for half seven to come round. I used to know, instantly, the sound of my mother's footsteps, as she walked up the ward corridor. My heart used to surge when I heard them but it would drop when the dreaded bell rang at half eight to signify that visiting time was over. My Ma always joked that I invariably seemed to need her to bring me in to use the toilet when the bell rang, just so that I could hang on to her for a few precious moments more. I never told her that not one night went by, that when the sound of her footsteps disappeared from the hospital corridor, I used sob and sob for her. I remember staring out at the big illuminated star that was the hallmark of the Star Cinema across the road from the hospital and feeling so alone. I knew that my Ma could see that star on the way to getting her bus and yet it felt as if we were a million miles apart.

I don't know whether it was because of the nurses assuming that I was mentally, as well as physically, handicapped or because I was so painfully shy, but I had very little interaction with the other patients and staff which merely served to heighten my loneliness.

This was really highlighted when the children in the ward used to receive basic school lessons. The teaching was supposed to make up for the education the kids were missing because they had to be in hospital. All the children used to sit around this portable blackboard while I lay in bed, more often than not with one or both of my legs covered in Plaster of Paris. The teacher used to ask them basic spelling or maths questions. Sometimes I knew some of the answers from what I had seen her teach previously but I was always too shy to speak them aloud, thus perpetuating the theory that my brain was also affected. My main memories of the hospital school are the feeling of being left out and longing to take part in it.

I remember on one particular stay in hospital I was in a room next to the nurses' station. The only other child in the room was a boy who I discovered was deaf, dumb and blind. For some crazy reason I was afraid of him. Not that the poor little guy could do anything to me, as he just lay there for much of the day. Maybe I feared that once you were in the disabled group then any potential disabilities might affect you and his looked to be just too horrific for me to cope with. Anyway, this kid always seemed to wait until the dead of night before he roused and started wandering around. More often than not he would wander towards the outside door of the room which led out to a balcony. Fortunately, the door was always locked and he would either make his way back to his bed or a nurse would notice him and bring him back.

One night he managed to either unlock the door or someone had left it open. He was about to go out on the balcony which was one floor up from the ground. I panicked and called out to the nurses who didn't hear me. I tried to manoeuvre myself in my bed in such a way that I could knock at the window to alert them but next thing I knew I'd fallen out of the bed! As I obviously hadn't got the callipers on I was fairly helpless on the ground. Hearing the commotion the nurses rushed in, brought the other kid safely back to his bed and then proceeded to give out to me for falling out of my bed. No wonder I hated the place so much!

Is it any surprise that my days were spent longing for that one hour visit from my mother to come around? How much more enlightened it is now that parents can come and go at will when visiting their children in hospital. I will always fervently wish that in my day parents had been allowed to spend as much time as they needed with their children. The old policy of strict one hour per session visiting was so destructive and so potentially psychologically damaging that it must have bordered, in my view, on abuse.

Such was the trust that my mother had in Doctors Regan and Brady that I don't think she ever fully explored the details of any surgery they proposed performing on me. She put my care completely in their hands, wholly believing that they would do right by me, as I'm sure they did. This was not because she didn't care or understand fully, she was always an incredibly tuned-in woman. It was merely an era which parents today would struggle to understand of "doctors know best".

Or maybe I'm doing her a disservice. In later years when I would ask her what all those many operations were designed to do or what surgical options had been put to her then, she always became so defensive. She'd say that she couldn't remember as it was such a long time ago. Even my extended family members don't know the specifics of the surgeries. The closest I've gotten is a memory one of my aunts has that my mother spoke to her at one point about an experimental surgery option being put to her when I was about one or two years old. It would either improve me or, apparently more likely, make me worse or even potentially kill me. According to my aunt, my mother declined. She never spoke about this to me. In my heart I knew she remembered and perhaps felt guilty in some way that the decisions she had taken, or perhaps not taken, had resulted in the difficulties that I would face all of my life. All I know, and in typical Irish male fashion I say it now that it's too late for me to be able to say it to her face, but guilt is the last thing she should ever feel about any decisions which she made for me. Instead she should feel pride – pride that she did her very best and for the very best reasons.

In some ways I'd love to know more about the operations. In my early 30s I began to feel the need to find out exactly what medical procedures were performed on me as a child. I rang the medical records section of Our Lady's to see if I could get a copy of my records only to be told that all records older than 25 years were destroyed. I have trawled through every other available source to find any of my hospital records from that time, which might throw some light on the surgeries, but it seems that all of the institutions followed the 25 year rule. Knowing that I could never look at my records made me feel as if all the sadness and loneliness that I had experienced while in that hospital had been for nothing. Had they not realised what I had gone through? Had they no record now of that little child, bereft of hope, lonely for his family and more importantly for the one gleaming light in his life, his mother? Would that I could have expunged the memories from my mind as easily as my medical records were expunged.

My Ma was really put out when she heard that I wasn't able to get hold of my records. Looking back, I think that she may have felt that this would have been official documentation outlining that she had done her best for me. I never did and never will need documentation confirming that.

I have always and genuinely felt guilty that my childhood recollections never gave due attention to the role which my father played. For that Da, I am truly sorry. Mammy used to tell me that he did come to visit me in hospital yet I can't remember it. But then I can't remember anyone visiting me but Mammy. I'm sure others did but my devotion and dependence on her was such that I seem almost to have blocked everyone else out from my memory. I do remember very clearly one time when I was discharged early from hospital unexpectedly. My brothers and my sister hid me in a tiny room at our back-door, where Mammy kept brushes and cleaning gear. When my father came home from work he said he was getting washed and ready to go up to see me in hospital. The others said they had a surprise for him. When they opened the door, I hobbled out. When he saw me, my Da clung on to me like he never did before or after – the sheer love of the embrace, I remember, filled me with guilt, even at that young age.

Up until then, in essence, I'd always felt that my Ma was my parents. Now, for the first time, I had let myself believe that I had two parents. Although it is hard for me to say this, I think also that for the first time, my Da truly acknowledged to himself that he had four children. It may not have been quite biblical in a prodigal son sense but he may have considered me lost in his heart but now I was found.

As Ma and Da worked, as well as spending so much time in hospital with me, I think that the other three had to become quickly self-sufficient. This must have meant that from the time they got home from school until either one of my folks came home they looked after themselves. I don't think it would have been allowed today, although the dangers which are around now generally didn't exist then. Liam maintains that he always got the dinner started which, because money was tight, was usually potatoes with beans or peas. Dominic and Anne are a bit hazier on this!

My Da was small of stature. He was only about five feet seven tall but because of the physical nature of his work, he was built like a brick shit-house. His muscles had muscles and I longed to look like him when I was older.

My father was what I suppose could be described as being self-taught. Like most children of his generation he left school at a very early age to find work to help his family out. He was the middle of three sons and had three sisters. Despite his early departure from school he was a voracious reader of books of all kinds and could more than hold his own in the company of more institutionally educated peers. He was one of the most learned men I've ever known. His only real social outlet was a few pints at the weekend after working hard as a builder's labourer during the week. Growing up, I remember he used to recount some of the discussions which took place around the bar in Downey's on Ballyfermot Road where the problems of the world were analysed and solved. It was obvious that his opinions were respected. After one of these brain-storming sessions he was telling me about how he had told this guy called "The Editor" that he was wrong about something.

"Why is he called the Editor?" I asked.

"Because every time he tells you something he always puts in 'Now to cut a long story short', so we nicknamed him The Editor."

Genius!

As a football nut, I was his oracle on any football questions which may have been flying around the pub. He always used to get pleasure telling the group the answer which I'd provided for him, especially on a question which may have stumped him and the rest of the pub.

"Now are you sure that's right Ger?" he'd always ask me.

Even in my earliest years of football mania I don't think I led him astray too often!

When I wasn't learning everything I could about football I was focussed on mastering the use of the callipers, with my mother's constant help. She had obviously determined that this needed to be done quickly so that I could attend mainstream school and integrate with other children.

At that young age it never occurred to me that this wouldn't be possible.

Two

GROWING PAINS

The first steps taken by a child are normally recorded at the months stage, mine were very much recorded in the years stage. I must have been five years old before I could fully master (if ever you can) the cumbersome, metal callipers which were to adorn my legs for life. Add to that mixture the utter discomfort and at times downright pain of them and you can understand just how determined I was to try to be like all the other children of my age. There was a huge population of us on Spiddal Road, Ballyfermot, in the late 1960s and all through the '70s. My abiding memory is of the many times that the thigh-length left leg calliper would break at the knee-lock joint. This lock enabled me to bend my leg when sitting down. I tried using a calliper which didn't have a knee lock – it was not pleasant. If you don't believe me try keeping one of your legs in a poker straight position for any length of time – it's tough and that's exactly how I found it. After sitting for any length of time when wearing the non-lock calliper, my leg would be so numb that when I stood up and it would take a while for the feeling to come back into it. Explaining this to other kids my age was never easy.

Pressure sores caused by wearing callipers were, and still are, an awful trial. The friction between the calliper and my thigh caused sores as big as a two euro coin. And you just had to, have to, wait until nature takes its course and the sore bursts before any sort of relief arrives.

But this is chicken-feed compared to the fear, or more accurately sheer unbridled terror, I had, and still have of the calliper breaking. The fear is that it will happen outside, leaving you unable to get to where you want to go, relying on others to carry, push, or use whatever possible means to get you to safety. Needless to say your pride, dignity, self-esteem and self-worth are so battered that it is little wonder that that fear has always been a dominant factor in my life.

The pain of a calliper breaking under you while you are walking is hard to describe. I've never been shot in the kneecap but it must be akin to the pain I used to go through when the calliper broke. If the calliper does break it will always be at its weakest point – the knee-lock joint. And when this happens, the pain literally rips through you, starting right at your kneecap and shooting up and down your leg. The pain is one which terrified me as a child. It happened so often too. The mixture of the poorly manufactured State-provided calliper and the extra weight which I carried, due to my lack of physical activity, was a recipe for the dreaded break to happen at any time. I remember coming up with the great discovery of taping ice-pop sticks to the sides of the calliper in order to strengthen it. I didn't seek a patent for this invention as I didn't find it very successful! I lived in such fear of the awful pain that I would have tried anything. Thankfully, the quality of the callipers has improved since I was a child so it hasn't happened for some time.

Strangely, one of the most inconvenient times that the calliper broke was on the morning of my brother, Liam's, wedding. I got up early, full of nerves as I was to be his Best Man and all the trauma that that job entails! I took a couple of steps that morning and the calliper broke. What a mad rush ensued! I had an old calliper, and boy do I mean old, which I put on. I virtually crawled out to my car so that I could bring the broken calliper to my saviour on so many occasions in my life, Kieran Hurley. Kieran has manufactured and repaired my callipers for more years than both of us care to remember. That Saturday morning, I sat in Kieran's sitting room, in his home in Ballinteer while he, still in his dressing gown, fixed the calliper for the big day ahead. Surreal!

When, as a child, the calliper did break it had to be brought to the Limb Fitting Clinic in the National Rehabilitation Hospital in Dun Laoghaire to be repaired. Again the curse of the scarcity of cars and public transport would intervene. The "vegetable man", Mr Tallon, who delivered vegetables to the convent where my Ma worked, also did deliveries around Dun Laoghaire so he would leave it in to the Clinic to be repaired and collect it when it was fixed. This would always take days to be done so, as I only ever had one calliper per leg, I was reduced to staying at home, crawling around on my hands and knees.

This only fuelled the frustration within me. Looking back, it was tough for a young kid to have to cope with. A young kid who just wanted to be normal, who wondered at times what he had done to deserve a life immersed in frustration and, at times, utter unhappiness. I remember all too often sitting, looking out of our front window, waiting for my Ma to come home from work and praying that she would have a large bag with her which would mean that my calliper was fixed. I had such a feeling of sadness when she used to arrive and tell me that the calliper was not yet fixed. God love her, it must have been as hard for her as it was for me.

And when the calliper wasn't broken, I tried as best as I could to integrate and play the games which the other kids played. Admittedly I had to do it at my level and at my pace. For instance, I was pretty crap at chasing and it took me so long to hide in "Hide and Seek" that I didn't pose too much of a challenge for my opponent!

I think every kid at that time used collect Football Cards. These were a pack of six cards with a piece of pink chewing gum inside and they cost a couple of pence. The taste of the chewing gum lasted for about a minute and after that you might as well have been chewing an elastic band! But the challenge of collecting the full set of cards kept us all going. And yet I don't think anybody managed to collect the full set, as there was always an elusive one. A clever marketing ploy or what!

One of the other highlights then was when the "Rag Man" came every week, collecting old rags and giving you a balloon or something of that sort in return. Ah the simple pleasures in life! Kids today would wet themselves laughing at the things we did for fun then.

But invariably, while I was involved in a major project like making a go-kart which John De Lorean would have been proud of, or collecting sticks which we would try to sell door to door, for people to use on their fires, the calliper would break thus rendering me housebound while I waited for it to be fixed. I lost count of the amount of times when my mother begged and pleaded for me to be given a second calliper which I could use while the other was being repaired only to be turned down by our caring Health Service. The only time they would consider an application for a new one was when you provided documentary proof that the original one was beyond repair. Former Health Minister Noel Browne would be spinning in his grave if he knew that such degrading practices went on in a health service that he cared so much about.

My Ma used to tell the story about bringing me to school one day when the calliper broke as we were crossing Ballyfermot Road. I had such a grip on her hand that I managed to bring her to the ground when I fell. But with gallantry belying my years, I screamed at the oncoming cars: "Don't knock my Mammy down!"

She said she struggled to get me up off the ground with the tears in her eyes. I'm sure they were tears of laughter but the sentimentalist in me hopes they were something else! But such was the morbid fear I had of anything happening to my Ma that I would have sacrificed myself ten times over for her. These fears weren't helped by the fact that well before she was 50 years old, Mammy's hair was totally grey. Even as a young child, I figured that Mammy looked older than she actually was because I was so much trouble to her. I thought that having to bring me back and forth to hospitals and generally spending so much time looking after me had turned her hair grey.

After much persuasion from her friends she finally decided to get a colour in her hair. This cheered me enormously as it made her look so much younger and convinced me that she would live forever! But, although I think she secretly loved this change in her appearance, she was such a reserved woman that instead of showing off her new hairstyle to the world, she constantly hid it behind a scarf. No amount of attempts to persuade her to ditch the scarf worked. I think, she felt that she was being too ostentatious by having what she would have considered to be a "younger person's hair". I never knew her to be anything other than that type of reserved person, when, in my eyes, whether she had grey hair or brown, she was just utterly perfect.

Mention of school affords me the opportunity to acknowledge the part that our Religious Orders played in my early schooling. Dominic, Anne and Liam all went to the nearby Mary Queen of Angels Primary School and I naturally assumed that I would be joining them there. My mother naturally assumed that I would too but when she went to enrol me there was an unexpected twist. The nuns in charge of the school told her that they were concerned that my callipers might mark their floors and so they wouldn't be able to accept me as a student there. My mother was still working in the laundry in the Dominican Convent, in the 'lower end' of Ballyfermot, over a mile from our home. When she told the nuns there what had happened they made immediate arrangements for me to go to their school – so I became one of the few boys from the 'upper end' of Ballyfermot to go to school in the 'lower end'. I hasten to say that we used, and still do use, these terms in a geographical rather than a pejorative sense lest I offend my fellow 'Ballyfermotites!'

I'm not quite sure what the other new school-goers made of me. I think they found it difficult to understand why, when they scurried around at a hundred miles an hour, I wasn't able to do likewise.

My first days in school were spent in such physical discomfort. At that time I was wearing the straight, no-lock calliper which meant that my leg was straight all day. I was conscious of Mrs Walsh telling us that we must stay in our seats unless we needed to go to the toilet. My leg quickly stiffened and would only be alleviated if I walked around. And yet I didn't need to go to use the toilet so had no reason to leave my seat. God love her, but Mrs Walsh would have been horrified to think I was sitting there in such pain and I didn't say anything! But, not for the first or last time, shyness and a determination to show that I was no different to anyone else prevented me from speaking up. The pain that I went through, particularly as the day wore on, was unmerciful and would leave me shattered at the end of the day.

Mrs Walsh was my first teacher in St Michael's School and she treated me with such kindness and affection. I remember being highly indignant when I was told that Mrs Walsh would eventually not be my teacher. I was even more shocked when I realised that I would have to move on to the De La Salle School, run by the Christian Brothers, further on down Ballyfermot Road. But that was years away then. In the meantime my Ma brought me to school everyday except for those days when I begged her not to, through notes which I used to leave for her pleading for her indulgence!

The two important events in a child's primary schooling,
or more accurately the two significant events in my era
of primary, were First Communion and Confirmation.
Before First Communion you had to go through your First
Confession. So our class was brought the short distance
from St Michael's School to Our Lady of the Assumption
Church. The schools in the Dominican Convent complex
were named after the Archangels, Michael, Gabriel, and
Raphael. We all sat in the pews outside the Confession box
and, of course, the first thing I noticed was that there was
a step up into the box. Now this step was hardly worth the
name, it was tiny and shouldn't have caused me a problem.
But I had myself so worked up over it that inevitably I
tripped up the step and fell into the Confessional and of
course, the kids outside started laughing. The priest rushed
out of the Confession box and hauled me up. He then
told me to get out of the House of God as I was making a
mockery of it. Looking back was I making a mockery of
the House of God or was He making a mockery of me?
Still trying to work that one out!

Funnily enough, it is only now that I realise that since
the priest threw me out of the church that I never did
get to make my First Confession so I must have received
my First Communion in a state of sin! However, I didn't
worry about that then. On the big day itself I was just so
relieved that I was able to use the Church's altar rail to
hold on to. It ran completely around the altar, thereby
allowing me to stand until the priest brought the Sacred
Host to me.

Sadly, Confirmation Day a few years later was a
different ball game. I quickly realised that it was going
to pose a problem as the Bishop who was to administer

the sacred oils of confirmation to the children, sat in a chair at the top of the altar, three steep steps up. I was barely ten years old when I made my Confirmation and, to this day, I remember the sick feeling in my stomach as I waited my turn to be called forward. As it was done alphabetically, I remember wishing beforehand that my surname started with an "A" so that I could get it over quickly or with a "Z" so that it could be put off for as long as possible! But "M" was literally slap bang in the middle!

I haven't a clue how I got up the steps to be confirmed by the then Archbishop of Dublin, Dermot Ryan. I remember the young church Curate, Father Wall, brought each child forward to the Archbishop, so he must have helped me. It is all lost in the haze of terror that I was in. I remember Father Wall saying to me when I got to the altar, "you look great," which gave me enormous encouragement.

As a family, we had always had a dog but that year, as a present for me successfully getting through my confirmation, I was allowed to have my own dog. So it was decided that when the Dominican Convent's dog, Scampi, a mongrel but predominately black Cocker Spaniel was having pups, I could have first pick of the litter. To describe myself as being excited just doesn't come close! The nun who looked after Scampi, Sister Cynthia, kept me informed of when I could expect the pups to arrive. My teacher in school at the time, Mr Carrick, gave out to me in no uncertain terms as I seemed to be always day-dreaming. And he was right!

And so, on October 18, 1972, (just how I remember the exact date I don't know!) the pups were born. I knew

which one of the six I wanted straight away. He was the
one who was completely black. And so "Brandy" arrived.
There was a song called "Brandy" by the O-Jays around at
the time so that's how he got his name! God I loved that
dog and he me. When it was time for me to come home
from school each day he used to sit outside my house and
when he would see me and Mammy getting off the bus
he would break the world land speed record in running
to me. He would be up around my neck, making such a
fuss, often knocking me to the ground!

One evening I noticed that Brandy was very quiet out
in the back garden. I made my way down towards the end
of the garden and noticed that he had his head stuck in
a breeze-block. There was hardly a sound coming from
him and it was obvious that he was in serious distress. I
panicked. Nobody knew what to do for the best. Lifting
the block up with him stuck in it might do him untold
harm. Just then, my Da arrived home. He had a couple
of pints on board and was slightly merry. He asked what
was wrong.

I couldn't get the words out but seeing how I upset I
was he said: "Don't panic Ger, I'll sort it."

I have to admit that I doubted that he could. He got a
hammer, walked towards Brandy and with the precision
of a surgeon, hit the block in a position where it split
perfectly in two. Brandy, now freed, was a bit dazed but
when he saw me he ran over to be comforted.

The surge of pride I felt for my Da was incredible.

I wish I could have told my Ma and Da how much
I hated my later years in primary school. Looking back,
I can find two reasons for this loathing – in primary
school I was bullied terribly, amongst others, by one boy

in particular. He was a nasty piece of work. Some years ago I heard that he had died tragically. God forgive me but when I heard this I thought 'Good enough for you' because he had made my life hell. At the time I didn't dare tell my parents as that, I thought, might only have made things worse. As a result of my reticence, his bullying tactics worked perfectly for him. I felt powerless. It taught me a lesson though that bullying, no matter how young or old the victim is, is one of the most horrible crimes against the person imaginable. Your physical and mental health is endangered, your reason for living a constant source of self-questioning. How I wish now that I had been stronger to put a stop to it or to have spoken to somebody who could have helped me.

But he thrived on my vulnerability. I couldn't run away from him, for obvious physical reasons, so I was literally a stationary target. And by God did he target. The bullying was not physical, just constant, in your face, never ending jibes about how I walked, how I looked and how sad and miserable he reckoned my life must be. And if I tried to walk away he would stand in front of me, blocking my way. So I would try to walk around him and inevitably with the physical and mental pressure that this would put me under, I would invariably fall, sending him into raptures of laughter. The strange thing is, like so many bullies, he was as thick as two short planks and so used his aggressive tactics to mask this. But he managed to gather a cohort around him to either egg him on or to imitate him in his absence.

And all the while I knew that I could never tell anyone about this as to do so would have meant my parents, or more probably my mother, going to the school demanding answers. As she was already bringing me to and from school, this would have made me feel further set apart from the other kids, so I kept quiet and hoped it would end. But the only days when I might have peace were when, for whatever reason, he was not in school. But invariably my prayers that he would be gone for an extended period from school were never answered and he would return refreshed, ready to resume the onslaught against me. Looking back, I am so ashamed of myself that I let him torment me for so long. But, in truth, what could I do? Walk away? Yeah right! In the time it took him to walk ten steps I could walk two. Fight him? One push from him and I would have been on the ground thus enduring further ridicule. No, I was well and truly up the creek without a paddle. Hopefully he has claimed his rightful place in Hell.

One other boy (whose name will be forever etched on my brain but who will remain nameless now for fear of litigation!) put himself firmly in a position in the school of being beyond bullying. Instead he was able to blackmail all of us into doing his homework for him. His modus operandi was that if you didn't do so he would simply puke on you. He had this ability to pinch some part of his throat which would immediately bring forth copious amounts of vomit! You did not mess with this guy. Short of bringing a pump-action shotgun into school, he was armed with the most lethal of weapons!

The second reason why I hated school was that while other kids eventually got to go to school by themselves or with their friends, my mother always brought me to school. This was mainly because of the distance involved. Now that's fine in the beginning but there comes a time when you don't want your Ma bringing you to school, as it doesn't exactly allow you to build up much street cred! I adored her and I can see why she did it but it only served to set me apart from my classmates, in my head at least.

The good part about Mammy working in the Dominican Convent was that I could walk to the convent, which was next door to the school, to meet my Ma at the end of the school day. While she worked away in the convent's laundry, she used to let me use the steam presser to iron smaller items of the nuns' clothing! I think I used to do a good job because I never saw her having to redo them or if she did, she did it very discreetly so as not to destroy my confidence. When all the clothes were washed and ironed, each nun had a number attached to their items and a vast wall in the laundry was filled with presses of pigeon-holes where all the clothes were filed away against their respective numbers. It's hard to believe that there were so many nuns in the convent then compared to the sparse amount which there are today. The convent no longer houses nuns as there are so few either still alive or preparing to become nuns.

One of the lasting memories I have of helping Mammy in the laundry was when she needed me to lend a hand folding the many bed sheets. I would sit at one end of the laundry and Mammy would give me one end of the sheet. Then she would walk to the other end of the laundry with her end of the sheet in hand. She would tell me to fold the sheet to the right. I would pretend that I didn't know my right from my left and turn it the opposite way. This used frustrate her no end. But I always knew that she'd never get angry with me. Instead, our chaotic bed sheet folding would leave the two of us laughing our heads off!

After our work was done we would get ready to go home. First though, we had to call into the kitchen to say goodbye to Sister Agnes, the first black person I ever met. I was transfixed when I met her first! I couldn't wait to tell everyone that I had actually met a black person. Sister Agnes was a lovely, burly nun, barely over five feet tall from Cape Town, South Africa. I was troubled by something about her for some time before eventually plucking up the courage to ask her: "Why is one side of your hand black as coal and the palm side as white as mine?

She said it was from all the time she spent washing the dishes! To this day I'm not sure if she was winding me up or not. I do know that Mammy told me many times afterwards not to be bothering Sister Agnes – a bit of a diplomat was my mother!

Spending time walking from school to the convent and helping Mammy when I got there, also gave me the chance to see the girl who was my first love. Looking back, I doubt very much if the attraction was mutual but I dreamed that it would be. Teresa was the only daughter of Mr Conroy, the caretaker, odd-job man, you name it he could do it, of the convent. The Conroys lived in a cottage in the convent grounds. Now God may have blessed me with legs which were about as useful as a handbrake on a canoe, but all other parts and emotions functioned very normally then, as they do now. God I was besotted with Teresa Conroy. I remember one of the women who worked with Mammy in the convent, Eileen Byrne, used to slag me incessantly about Teresa. I pretended to be mortified but secretly I was delighted as it made me feel like every other boy – I wasn't Gerard the disabled boy, I was Gerard the boy who had it so bad for this girl. I remember buying Teresa a box of chocolates for Christmas one year when I was at most 11 years old and she the same. What a romantic fool I was!

Come to think of it, over 30 years later, I'm still the same!

THREE

INTO THE WAR ZONE

Somehow I toughed out the years of primary school and came through it relatively unscathed. I knew, though, that secondary school was going to be a whole new ball game and by God I was right. St John's College Secondary School, Ballyfermot, again a Christian Brothers school, was at most times akin to being caught up in a war zone.

Before starting in St John's, the Summer of 1974 was filled with the simple question: "How was I going to actually get there?" It was a little over half a mile from home, which made it too far for me to walk and too short to be a bus distance, even if it was covered by a bus route which it wasn't. Primary school for all its failings and terrors did have the useful practicality of being handy to a bus stop. So I broached the subject with Mammy and the only solution was to get a wheelchair which she would push me to school in every day. It really was the only solution and I reluctantly agreed. In my heart I knew it was such a demonstrable move which would surely only serve to separate me further from my school-mates.

At that time Liam was working in a garage before doing his apprenticeship in car mechanics, so he got me loads of stickers from various motoring places which I put on the chair to jazz it up a bit. It was an attempt to make it feel more like a Formula One car than a wheelchair! And, in fairness, it did look different. But there was no getting away from it. No matter how much I dressed it up or tried to camouflage it, a wheelchair is a wheelchair is a wheelchair and I wasn't expecting to see many of my future classmates having to use one.

During the summer between the end of primary school and the beginning of secondary school, one sunday afternoon, myself and Mammy went down to the school to check things out. It was the maiden voyage for the wheelchair. I felt awful at having to use it but my preoccupation with those thoughts was quickly superseded by other worries when we got inside the school grounds. I nearly shit myself when I saw it. I wasn't shocked by the imposing Monastery overlooking it, where the Brothers lived, or by the playing fields surrounding it. No, what immediately struck me were the four steps leading up to the porta-cabin facilities. I knew this was where the first, second and third year students were based, as they worked towards the Intermediate Certificate exams. There was no handrail on the steps so I would have to figure out how I was going to overcome this. I remember sitting at the bottom step and thinking that just when I had worked out a compromise of sorts on how I was actually going to get to the school, now a further obstacle was being put in my way. 'Somebody up above must be taking the piss,' I thought.

In the end I concluded that there was only one solution. I would stand at the side of the steps and try to hoist my right leg, my 'good leg,' to the top of them and then crawl to my feet. When the school day was over I would literally sit on the ground at the top of the steps, regardless of whether it was wet or dry, and drop myself over the side of the steps, again landing on my 'good leg'. This was done while my Ma scrambled the wheelchair either up or down the steps. My embarrassment at this daily ritual was huge. I'd like to say that it lessened with time but it didn't. Mammy used to say that it would be easier if she helped me up the steps but I refused as I wanted to show my classmates that I had a modicum of independence. In any event, I was terrified that if I let Mammy help me up the steps I might stumble and possibly bring her crashing down.

So for five years of Secondary schooling, Mammy pushed me down to school every morning, went on to do her work in the convent and then brought me a flask of soup at lunchtime while all the other lads went home for their lunch. I think the soup was my Ma's way of checking in to make sure I was alright as a packed lunch was never once suggested as an alternative! She would then collect me when school ended at 4.05 pm, every afternoon. As by this stage, Dominic had gone on to Third Level and Anne and Liam was starting on their careers, I couldn't even get them to bail me out! Indeed, Dominic's influence had further consequences. He had attended St John's a few years previously and had obviously been one of the star pupils. So much so that on my arrival at my new school, the head brother, Brother Austin, said to me: "You've a lot to live up to. Dominic was one of the brightest students we've ever had here."

No pressure then! This glowing reputation came back to haunt me a couple of years later when the Irish class got some really stiff homework. At that time, I was intent on having fun, especially playing football, and homework was an inconvenience. On that night I asked Dominic if he would do this particularly tricky homework for me. This he duly did and the next day each person stood up, one by one, to give their answer and each one in turn was worse than the other. The teacher was getting more exasperated by the minute when it finally came to my turn to deliver.

Dominic's prepared answers hit the spot. I was saying Irish words that I hadn't used or heard, before or since.

When I was finished, the teacher said: "Well done Maguire. Excellent answer. It's good to see that Dominic hasn't lost his excellent grasp of his native tongue."

A clear case of defeat snatched from the jaws of victory!

Going to and from school myself and Mammy lost count of the amount of downpours which the Irish winters visited upon us. We got drenched so often. Invariably Mammy always went over the top in ensuring that I was as covered up as possible, without caring too much for herself.

During my first years in Secondary School, my father had been made redundant from work. Jobs were just so scarce in the mid-1970s that despite his best efforts he was struggling to get another one. So sometimes he would come down to the school to meet me when it was over. One day he was late so I started to make my own way, knowing that I would meet him before long which I did about 100 yards from the school passing by the County Bar pub. He was carrying a big bag of potatoes and said: "Will you get out of the chair for a while and we'll put the potatoes in?"

So I naturally got up and gave a poor old lady passing by such a fright. When she saw me standing up from the wheelchair she nearly fainted and said: "Jaysus it's a miracle!"

The miracle at the shrine outside the County Bar pub in Ballyfermot never did hit the national headlines!

Summer holidays from school were wonderful. The weather was always fantastic – that's not an old wives' tale or looking back with rose-coloured glasses – it was. It was a time when myself and all the others of my age played football on the road or on the field across the road from my house. We'd be out from early morning 'til late at night. Matches were played using more of a snooker scoring system – first to ten wins or sometimes first to a lot more. Matches would last for hours. As soon as one finished, another one would begin.

Now I'm no fool. Whilst I dreamed of being Peter Osgood or Alan Hudson or Charlie Cooke, (you'd never guess I was as mad a Chelsea supporter then as I am now would you!) I knew that when my friends where picking teams they used to pick me with the intention of playing me in a position where I could do least harm. I take no offence in that. In fact some well-known professional players have made a fortune with a similar reputation! As I was big-boned (no I was not fat, I was big-boned!)

I managed to hone my goalkeeping skills. Whilst I was determined to model myself on the Chelsea goalkeeper, Peter "The Cat" Bonetti, if I was honest my movements in goal were tortoise-like rather than cat-like. However, I could never be accused of ever giving less than 100 per cent.

I was always so inwardly furious with friends who were into things like chess or other pastimes which didn't require two good legs! 'Why couldn't I have their legs and they could have mine? If I had their legs I could play all sports, all day long, I used to think. However, I was well and truly stuck with what I had.

In later years, when I told my brother Liam this he said that he often wished as a child that I could have his legs for a day so that I could see what life with "proper" legs was like. But, as I said to Liam when he told me this, one day would not have been enough for me! For on the rare occasions that I found myself playing out-field and managed to bundle in a goal (no 25 yard screamers for me!) the feeling of exhilaration was such that he would never have gotten his legs back.

I actually scored from a penalty on one occasion. The fact that I had been entrusted with the penalty must have been because my team had a fairly healthy lead at the time. If truth be told, just as I came up to strike the ball, I slipped on the wet grass but in so doing I made beautiful contact with the ball and it flew passed the goalkeeper. I think everyone was a bit surprised at my prowess. I didn't let on that it was a complete fluke! Oh that John Terry could have had such luck in Moscow in 2008!

One memory which lives with me 'til this day is a match we were playing for hours – first to 20 wins. It was

locked at 19-19, I was in goal. You may scoff and say I
had let in 19 goals in one match but then so did the fella
in the other goal and he wasn't lugging around a couple
of stones of metal on his legs was he? It could have
been the Maracana in Rio or the San Siro in Milan but
it couldn't have been tenser than it was on "The Green"
on Spiddal Road. Despite conceding 19 goals, I wasn't
having such a bad game – at 19-19 though I was praying
that I wouldn't make a mistake which might cost us the
marathon match. The opposition came forward, a shot
came in from distance and somehow I let it spill through
my hands. It was more of a pass back than a shot if I'm
honest and I don't think it was exactly Peter Lorimeresque,
but it crept just inside the near jumper. There was nothing
as fancy as goal posts in our day! We'd lost. Everyone
walked off, the match forgotten within seconds. The next
match was already being planned. I, however, felt as if
I'd been responsible for conceding a last minute goal in
the FA Cup Final, European Cup Final and World Cup
Final all rolled into one. The reverberations of it may not
have shook the football world but (are you listening Roy
Keane?) this was my Saipan!

This was the era of one channel television. RTÉ came
on air in the evening and finished broadcasting at around
11.30 pm. So there was no lounging around watching TV
all day. In truth, watching a small screen, black and white
television which broke down with incredible regularity,
was not too enticing. Multi-channel TV (just the BBC and
ITV, not the hundreds of channels available today) was
installed on Spiddal Road the day before the World Cup
in West Germany in 1974 started. All of us kids stared at
the guys who were up ladders installing the cables with

gratitude and awe. It was as if they were delivering food to the starving masses! The thought of wall-to-wall football was almost a miracle. Almost!

And when the weather got too bad for real football to be played, artificial football, in the form of Subbuteo, came forward. Mini-tournaments among the kids on the road took place and the great thing was that my team was the same as everyone else. There were no barriers here. If only all sport could have been played on a piece of green cloth!

When I wasn't out enjoying myself, as a family of six, we were like other families at that time, living on a day-to-day basis. Money was extremely short and at times, I am sure, non-existent. Parents went without to ensure that their children were properly fed and watered.

We had one secret weapon to help us get through some of the freezing cold nights when there was no easy way of heating the bedrooms. My father had been in the Royal Air Force during the war with his time being served in base camps rather than in the air. Considering that he was only 20 years old when the war ended, he obviously joined up to send money home to his own parents and their young family, rather than to rid the world of Nazi or Fascist forces. He had brought home a big brown, serviceman's overcoat from the war. Now whether he was actually meant to do this may be another story! So this big coat was used by each of us kids in turn at bedtime, the way a warm duvet would be used today. Looking back, Da was only about five feet seven or eight inches tall so this coat must have been down to his ankles. But by God did it keep us warm on cold nights!

He also brought home this big suitcase which us

kids were warned never to go near. We wondered and speculated so many times about what could possibly be in it. But as a child I was wary of looking at it, never mind looking inside it, as my Da was so insistent on us never opening it. When he died, my mother did open it and found all the letters he had written to his mother from the war. Our grandmother had kept them and he obviously reclaimed them when she died. I asked my Ma what was in the letters and she was highly indignant that I should ask about them.

"They were private between your father and his mother so I burned them," she said.

God, I wish that I could have been that honourable.

My father and his coat very nearly never made it back home from the war. He came close to being killed in a bizarre incident when an RAF plane crash-landed at the base where my father was stationed. On seeing the plane in obvious difficulties, my father and some others ran to take cover behind a few large barrels. They watched as the plane careered towards the ground. Sadly, it hit at full force and pieces of the plane went flying everywhere. When everything calmed down my father came out from behind the barrels. It was then he noticed that they were marked 'DANGER – HIGHLY FLAMMABLE'. His lucky escape was not shared by those on the plane who all perished.

* * * *

In September 1975, myself and Mammy went on a pilgrimage to Lourdes.

She had suggested the trip to me some months

previously. I think she expected me to baulk at the idea
but I saw something major coming out of this. In my
naivety I was absolutely convinced that I was going to
come back cured. I had all my friends convinced too! I had
read stories and had heard so many accounts of miracles
happening there that curing me of my disability seemed
a mere formality. On a more practical level, a few days
spent getting cured in Lourdes also meant a few days less
that I had to spend in dreaded school.

I made so many plans of what I was going to do when
I came back cured. I had always played such a good game
of football in my head, now I was actually going to be able
to transfer this to my feet! I was going to be able to ride a
bike. Chopper bikes were all the rage. I could, maybe, get
one for Christmas. And as for girls! They would see me in
a completely different light. God I was going to be such a
babe magnet when I came back from Lourdes cured!

I don't know where Ma and Da got the money for this
trip. One thing is certain, though, it can't have been easy.
It probably cost more then to travel abroad than it does
now. There were none of your one cent plane journeys
then. We travelled with the Cystic Fibrosis Association
of Ireland pilgrimage. Why, I'm not sure. All I know is
that we met one of the organisers of the pilgrimage about
a year later in Our Lady's Hospital and she told us that
many of the children who had been on the pilgrimage had
died in that intervening year.

The journey to Lourdes was awesome. It was my first
time to go to Dublin Airport never mind go on a plane!
Looking back, the way the mobility impaired passengers
were boarded onto the plane was extraordinary. We were
loaded onto the baggage lifts and hoisted up to the door

of the plane. It was so undignified. I wonder is it too late to sue the airline for psychological damage caused! I'd like to think that such indignities would not happen today but alas I'm sure they do. We can send satellites to Mars yet we can't manage to organise disabled people onto aircraft without it being a major hassle.

I wish that someone had warned me beforehand that once the plane was airborne, you get the feeling that it has actually stopped in mid-air and is not actually moving. I got such a fright. 'What a time to die,' I thought. 'I'm on my way to ridding myself of my disability and we are about to plough into the sea below!' I remember Mammy looking at me and we both had this sort of 'Is this supposed to be happening?' look on our faces. Thankfully, we quickly noticed that things on the ground were moving and the potential disaster, as we saw it, was averted!

When we got to Lourdes Airport, which was no more than an airfield then, a lot of us literally had to arse our way down the steps of the aircraft. It must have looked like something out of a Marx Brothers movie!

Alas, within a few days, all of my hopes and dreams of leaving my disability behind in Lourdes were dashed. Despite going on all the torchlight processions and being immersed in the freezing cold water of the baths, my gift from God was to remain with me. I remember myself and Mammy sitting before Our Lady's Grotto one night, as the lines of people of all varying nationalities went up to kiss the sacred statue. I felt singularly uneasy at having to do this and literally had to be pushed out of my seat by my mother when it was my turn to go up. Mammy told me that no sooner was I back in my seat having kissed the statue than I was up again, heading up to kiss it once more. To this day I don't know what propelled me to do this or maybe I do and I just don't want to admit it.

I came back from Lourdes slightly disappointed at not being cured, but hugely relieved that my disability was not as bad as some of the disabilities I saw there. Some of the scenes of utter human misery were so terrible to view. How those people coped with the disabilities they had was far too difficult for my young mind to compute. The poverty of hope which I witnessed in Lourdes was astonishing. Seeing people, so badly disabled, being ferried around in glorified wheel-barrows, really shook me. There were people there with such profound disfigurements that despite my best efforts not to stare at them, I undoubtedly did. Misery manifested itself in so many faces. These people were all hoping that their faith might bring them, not so much a better quality of life, but just a quality of life.

I told my mother that I factored down my prayers when I went to the Baths where you kiss the statue of the Blessed Virgin Mary. As you're in sub-zero water temperatures, you express your hopes and prayers. I felt so guilty asking to be cured after witnessing such abject suffering and misery that instead I just asked for Chelsea to win their next league game. As a matter of interest, my altruism fell on deaf heavenly ears as Fulham beat Chelsea 2-0 the following Saturday!

In any event, I was fascinated that one of the stories which I heard before going to Lourdes actually turned out to be true. I'd been told that the minute you got out of the baths you were bone-dry. There was no need for towels – nothing. Within seconds I was dry and putting my clothes back on. And believe me, my Ma was so protective of me that she wouldn't have allowed me to do that unless I was completely dry!

The journey to Lourdes, therefore, was not a wasted one. It made me realise that how I was, and how much I felt it, was bad, but I came home thinking that it could have been so much worse.

I wouldn't go as far as to say that what I had seen in Lourdes had had a 'Road to Damascus' sort of conversion effect on me, but it did change me for a time, even at that young age. I took consolation from the fact that I had at least finished my first year in Secondary School. Okay, I had done so in a fairly unorthodox way and my pride had had to be back-pocketed every day. But nobody could deny the fact that I had done it. So I remember making a conscious decision when I got back from Lourdes to just get on with it in my second year and to remember that at least I was able to get to school, albeit in a vastly different way from my schoolmates. I also thought that the novelty of seeing me crawling up steps or being pushed in a wheelchair had to be gone by now. And so with the strain of the mental torture that I had been putting myself through slightly salved, second year wasn't as bad as the first.

By my third year all I was thinking about was that my first major academic examination was on the horizon. However, with my burgeoning fantasy football career in progress, preparation for my Intermediate Certificate Examination in 1977 was less than thorough. At that time it was considered that if you passed five out of the eight or nine exams that you sat, then you were deemed to have passed your Inter Cert. So I convinced myself that getting five "Ds", forget about honours, would be a piece of cake.

However, unsurprisingly, given the pathetic amount of studying which I did for the exams, I failed my Inter Cert miserably. I got a good mark in my English Exam though. In the composition section I'm fairly sure I broke the world record for mentioning that I was disabled as many times as possible. What kind of hard-hearted examiner would not be moved by that, I thought!

That Summer of 1977 was a scorcher. But I couldn't really enjoy it as I had a constant knot in my stomach at what I just knew were going to be my impending Inter Cert results. If I had known just how disappointing they would turn out to be, that knot would have turned into a bowling ball!

Failure in my Inter Cert hit me hard. For the first time, my mother's gloves came off. I remember being in tears when I got my pathetic results and she said to me in no uncertain manner that life was going to be tough enough for me in the future without me making a mess of important exams. The late 70s was a time of economic gloom in Ireland. I was going to find it hard enough to persuade employers to give me a chance without lousy exam results in my back pocket, she told me. Remember, this was a time when equality legislation was unheard of. The book was very much judged by its cover and I knew that I was always going to be playing catch-up when it came to applying for jobs. I think Mammy's laying down the law was her way of voicing her concerns. She had always walked with me, and would continue to do so, but there was coming a time, sooner rather than later, when I would have to go it alone.

My misery at failing my Inter Cert and my terrible results was compounded on the first day back in school in the September following the exam. The new head brother of the school, Brother Benignus, gathered all of us new fifth years in the sports hall. He told those who had failed the Inter Cert to separate themselves from the others and to walk to the opposite end of the hall.

If ever I wanted the ground to open up and swallow me it was then. Mercifully, I wasn't alone in making that long walk. I was, however, the slowest and the noisiest. When I walk, my left foot comes down with something akin to a thud. That thud, in a large sports hall, on wooden floors, was like singular blows to my gut. Jesus how I wished I could walk faster (and quieter). And yet I knew if I tried to walk faster than I normally did that there was a danger that I would fall, thus heightening my shame of myself. However, instead of this public flagellation making me become a source of ridicule to my classmates, I sensed such a feeling of camaraderie from the silence that hung in that hall. It was as if the wagons had been circled.

Brother Benignus's attempts either at some sort of motivation, or, more likely knowing the man concerned, public humiliation, had back-fired on him. All of us boys, who went on to become the Fifth and Sixth Year Leaving Cert class of 1979 turned on him and made his life a misery for the next two years.

The most popular lad, by far, in the class was David Hickey. He took me under his wing and we became great buddies. It was a friendship which to my regret we didn't maintain when we went our separate ways after the Leaving Cert exams. We became the Morecambe and Wise, the Two Ronnies, the laugh a minute guys, for the next two years whilst also getting some serious study in. We were compared to the two old lads on the 'Muppet

Show' at the time! We were both prodigious arm-wrestlers
and kept the class transfixed on many occasions by our
arm-wrestling contests. Looking back, those Leaving Cert
years of 1977-1979 were so enjoyable. They may not have
seemed it at the time though. But I don't believe that you
can ever replicate the feeling of camaraderie that you have
in your school days.

Having said that it was dog eat dog at times too and
those days were horrendous for some boys. I witnessed
bullying of a vicious and savage nature, by both staff and
other pupils. But you watched. You never, ever raised your
head above the parapet to say "stop". You just thanked
God that you weren't on the receiving end and instead
felt sorry for the poor sods who suffered. I used to think
back to my primary school days and the misery I suffered
being bullied then and I swore that I was not going to go
through that again. Strangely I wasn't touched by bullying
in all my years in secondary school – why I honestly don't
know. This was just as well because in truth this bullying
was of a much more serious and sinister nature.

I remember being horrified at the practice of grabbing
a first or second year lad from the corridor and kicking
them so hard where boys just shouldn't be kicked. Then
they'd be thrown back out into the corridor. Of course,
you laughed at it, even though, deep inside you, you knew
that this was so wrong. But "better him than me," was
how I, and all the others who kept quiet, felt about it. The
tension which hung in the air while these guys waited to
pounce on an unsuspecting victim was horrible. It took an
instance of a young lad requiring surgery to rectify one of
these attacks to finally stop the practice. So when I said it
was akin to a war zone, I wasn't joking. I took solace from

the fact that neither myself nor Dave Hickey ("Sharky" – I never knew why!) took any part in it. We just wanted to have a laugh and be laughed at!

In the 1970s, Ireland was very much mono-cultural. I can remember that we had a young lad from Northern Ireland, Thomas McVicar, in our class for a few weeks and it eventually got round that he was actually a Protestant. I swear that people actually began to fear him when this became known!

We also had a black fella in our class. This would be completely the norm today. In the mid-1970s it was anything but. He had a broader Ballyfermot accent than I had! One day, he was bringing his homework up to the teacher when the teacher shouted at him as he was going back to his desk: "Come back here nigger."

The teacher made an apology to him in front of the whole class the next day. Could you imagine the national furore this would cause if this were to happen today? And rightly so.

We also had a fella, Dermot, in our class who had the most terrible stammer. A nicer, more intelligent bloke you would struggle to meet and very helpful to us, his more intellectually-challenged classmates! One day, the Brother who taught us Irish, Brother Michael, brought in a tape recorder. He said he was going to record us all speaking Irish. Instantly, all our thoughts centred on Dermot. We were incredulous that the Brother was seriously thinking of doing this. He started the recordings as far away from Dermot as he could have. This only served to increase Dermot's nervousness which was bound to make his stammer become even worse. The tension which the rest of us felt for him was palpable. When it came to his turn, our fears, and I'm sure his worst, were realised. It was awful and was compounded when Brother Michael proceeded to play back the recording to the whole class. It served no purpose educationally other than to deliberately humiliate someone.

Secondary school was also the time when sport became more competitive for young fellas of my age. The friendly kick-around which I did my best to take part in with my friends on the field across from my house was one thing but there wasn't a snowball's chance in hell of me being able to step up to this new mark. The knowledge of that fact used to kill me. I would see my classmates playing soccer or basketball for the school and I would feel so utterly frustrated that I couldn't be a part of it. As I said before, in my head I was then and am now the most fantastically gifted footballer! Playing in there I can perfect the Johan Cruyff turn, the Pele dribble or the Denis Law header. Transmitting this to my sorry excuses which passed for legs was another ball game!

I know that I let that frustration eat away at me which only served to make me unhappier. It was such a frustrating time all round – frustration at not being able to compete in the sporting arena and also in the romance arena. I saw lovely girls hanging around with blokes who were real shits and was so aggravated that they would be with them and never give me a second glance. "I would be so much better to her than him" was my constant moan to myself. Yet what girl at that time was going to take the dramatic step and go out with the disabled bloke, no matter how damned handsome I was! It all served up to feed me with a constant dish of frustration, frustration, frustration.

My Inter Cert results had taught me one thing though. To get any way half-decent Leaving Cert results, I was going to have to seriously get my arse in gear. And I did. I became almost hermit-like. I studied and studied until I could study no more.

The exams finally came around and I completed my Leaving Certificate exams in the Summer of 1979. I tried to put them out of my mind as I waited for the results but it was tough. I consoled myself with the thought that even if the results turned out to be rubbish, I had put in the time. I had, at least, given it my best shot.

When the day finally arrived, the feeling of trepidation I felt when I went to collect the results was incredible. I knew that failure would have such far reaching consequences for me. I was ecstatic when I opened the envelope and saw that I had passed the obligatory five subjects. I couldn't wait to show my Ma. That piece of paper was the evidence of both of our years of toil and struggle. My ecstasy was without doubt matched by hers when she saw my results.

This was the pre-points for third-level education era. This is just as well as I don't think totting up my points would have proved too taxing an exercise. I was so pleased when I passed though, albeit passing the bare minimum five subjects. I was so delighted that I could give something tangible back to Mammy for all that she had put in.

And, as pleased as I was with my results, the best was yet to come. Finishing school allowed me to rid myself of the wheelchair, without which, I have to admit, it would have been a logistical nightmare to negotiate getting to and from school. To this day, I can't remember how I actually physically got rid of the chair. I have a vague recollection that I asked Liam to dump it for me. Despite how functionally beneficial it was, I hated it and just wanted it expunged from my life.

After I'd got over my joy at finishing school it was time to move on with my life. I knew that Mammy had been laying the foundations all those years, but now it was up to me to find work. Upon leaving school, I started receiving DPMA (Disabled Persons Maintenance Allowance) of IR£20 (€25) per month. That wasn't going to take me far. I had no clue what I wanted to do or what I was able to do. One thing was obvious though. I knew that I needed to have my own transport. It was clear I wouldn't be able to drive a "normal" car, so the apron-strings went back on and Mammy made arrangements for me to take driving lessons in the Irish Wheelchair Association in Clontarf. I have to confess that I hadn't a clue where Clontarf was. Myself and my Ma went to Blackheath Drive every Wednesday for six weeks in late 1979. In April 1980, after only a few lessons, I'm proud to say, I passed my Driving Test at the first attempt. I was so proud, yet a woman who 17 and a half years earlier had been advised to forget about this new potential driver, was prouder still.

And so I was ready to take my place in the adult world, armed with my newly acquired licence! And then two thoughts struck me: Where the hell was I going to get a job? And where the hell was I going to get the money to buy this car that I was now licensed to drive?

It was time for all the family to put our collective heads together, to try to come up with a solution.

FOUR

ROLES REVERSED

The Celtic Tiger's' mother was only in school when I set out on my journey to find work in 1979. That journey would take me close on two years. In those long days I gave thought, for the first time, to how bleak and unpromising my life was becoming and the merits for continuing with it.

When I got my Leaving Cert results in August 1979, I had naively thought that before the start of the new decade, I would be a fully paid-up member of the country's workforce. Then the 1980s arrived. Ireland was in the grip of an incredible recession and despite my best efforts, I found that nobody was willing to give me a chance. I could have papered the walls of my home with letters of applications for jobs sent and the rejections received. I was careful to only apply for jobs which I was sure that I would be physically able to do. I saw no point in setting my sights too high. That was not a sign of any lack of ambition on my part but more of an acknowledgment of the constraints which my disability placed upon me and the economic pressures which prevailed at the time. I was not being magnanimous towards any future employer. I just did not want to run the risk of compromising myself. I set my sights low – basic clerical, photocopying, filing, short-term perhaps, rung on the ladder stuff. A job which would allow me to get a few bob together to buy an old banger of a car and also pay for the insurance – insurance which had a very heavy "disability loading" on it. Again this was a sign of the times. Crazily, in order to qualify for any State grants to help me buy a car, I had to have a job. And yet how was I going to find a job without a car?

During all the interviews, I began to despise my disability, if it were possible, more and more. So much of the interview time was taken up with questions about it, resulting, invariably, with me almost pleading to be given a chance. The most memorable incident was when I applied for a job, coincidentally, in a firm in Ballyfermot. I had persuaded my mother that it was time that I used public transport, such as it was at that time, by myself. So, without doubt reluctantly, she agreed. I got the bus to the interview and walked the short distance to the firm – to this day their name is etched on my brain and I still think of the way I was treated there each time I pass their premises today. A man, who later introduced himself as the owner, and a lady, who turned out to be his secretary, were standing at a window at the front of the business as I walked towards it. If there's one thing which will make a disabled person feel more conscious of how they walk, it is someone staring at them while they do so. That day, I was stared at with gusto by these two. When I got inside, I said I was there for an interview for the clerk's job.

The manager mumbled something to the secretary and he then said to me: "Oh that job was filled a few days ago."

I showed him the letter inviting me for an interview that day. It was signed by him.

He said: "Oh right, well I'll interview you for the practice if you like."

Like a fool, I went along with the charade with a lump in my throat. After the pointless interview, he ushered me on my way. The advertisement for the position of a clerk in that company stayed in the newspaper for some weeks afterwards.

My routine every day during those two years was the same. I had a free bus pass during off peak times due to my disability, so every morning I took the 78 bus into Fleet Street, walked from there to the offices of ANCO (now Fás) on D'Olier Street, to see if any jobs which I could apply for had appeared on their notice board. I regularly applied for anything that came up, but without success. I was registered with the National Rehabilitation Board (NRB) whose role was to help people with a disability to find employment. Even with their expertise and guidance, I found nothing.

I felt so lost during this time. I saw my brothers and sister working. Dominic had qualified as a Telecommunications Engineer and was working for a company in Tallaght, Anne was working in PMPA Insurance Company and Liam had finished his apprenticeship as a Motor Mechanic.

My father, despite losing his job through redundancy

after 28 years service with a building firm, with what can only be described as a pathetic pay-off, had found himself a job in Beechams of Ireland and my mother was still working in the Dominican Convent. I felt as if I was sponging off everyone although nobody made me feel like that. They were as concerned for me as I was.

I remember going to my GP, Dr Forde, just to speak aloud my fears. I sobbed like a baby in front of him. We talked for over an hour. His words of consolation and encouragement helped considerably. I'm sure that he doesn't remember, or even have a record of that visit, but just voicing my fears aloud together with his words of encouragement kept me going. It made me see that I just had to keep persevering. Had I not spoken to him as frankly and as honestly as I did, I believe that the depths of depression I was in would, sooner rather than later, have driven me to put a stop to a life which I believed more and more was beyond hope or meaning.

And so I applied for more and more jobs, went for the interviews when called, and knew that no matter how well I performed it wasn't going to be enough. The one thing that all the employers took away with them was that I was disabled. This led to the inevitable question, did they really need the hassle of employing a disabled person.

My NRB rep, Noeleen, kept me informed of all job possibilities and I pursued them vigorously, but to no avail. She brought me to ANCO in Ballyfermot to see what courses I could potentially do. I decided that I wanted to do a Cabinet Maker's course. I'm sure the course organiser nearly shit himself when I decided upon this and he probably had some sleepless nights about it. But fate was to intervene and save him and, probably, me!

Finally in late 1980, Noeleen told me that the Civil Service were introducing a 3 per cent quota of disabled people within their workforce. The employment drive was to coincide with the International Year of Disabled People. Whilst I applied and competed for jobs which were open to anyone, I have to admit that I was a little reluctant to apply for a job which, as I saw it, was specifically targeted at disabled people. I was sure that I would be capable of cutting it with able-bodied people – I just wanted a chance to prove it. But my back was well and truly to the wall and I knew that I would regret it for a long time if I didn't take this chance. She advised caution, however, because, although I may have felt as if I was the only disabled person in the country desperately looking for work, there were thousands of people in the same position as me. In reality 3 per cent of the Civil Service workforce did not equal thousands.

I took that on board but couldn't stop myself from feeling hopeful. The competitor in me also came to the fore. I knew by the statistics which Noeleen had put before me that I would have to play a stormer like I had never done before, if I was to be part of the successful 3 per cent. So with everyone praying and doing Novenas to all kinds of saints, I decided to give it one hell of a go.

I applied and sat my exams for the position of Clerical Assistant a few weeks later. The exam was held in the Central Remedial Clinic in Clontarf – the hall was packed with people with varying disabilities, the vast majority of whom must have felt, as I did, that we were all drinking in the last chance saloon.

That journey to Clontarf was my first journey driving alone in my extremely second hand Renault 12. I had bought it with every penny which I and the rest of my family could muster. My insurance actually cost more than the car – inflated with that very hefty disability loading. How times have changed! The car actually broke down on the way home from the exam, in Ballybough. I remember thinking 'Thank God it was on the way home. Imagine if it had happened on the way there and I had missed the exam.' I think that that would have finished me altogether!

I soon realised that the handbrake had become jammed. Now my lower body may be nothing to boast about but at least I do have good upper body strength. So much so that one of my bosses in later life once said to me that if he had had my shoulders he could have hit a golf ball 300 yards down the fairway! When I suggested that he take my legs too the deal suddenly didn't seem so appetising to him! But despite whatever strength I may have had, I just could not budge this handbrake but fortunately this all happened outside a garage. A mechanic there worked on the car for over half an hour, refused to take a penny for doing so and wished me well. Surely the omens were stacking up in the right direction!

I was delighted to hear that I had successfully passed the exams, as was my Ma. I was then called for an interview, which took place in Hawkins House, formerly the Theatre Royal. One of the questions I remember being asked was what special arrangements would I need to be put in place if I were being considered for the position. I remember feeling a bit pissed off at the question and replied: "Well I went through 12 years of schooling without needing anyone to put any special arrangements in place for me, so I don't see why I should need any now."

A tad cheeky and maybe petulant, but it must have worked because on March 31, 1981, I began my Civil Service life in the Department of Health, again in Hawkins House. And, over 28 years later, they still can't manage to get rid of me!

* * * *

When I started work, for the first time in my life I felt utterly independent. My Ma had carried me both figuratively and literally for all of my life yet now, I stood alone. I was working, earning a wage, paying my way, and most importantly being and feeling like an equal. I got a salary advance of IR£40 (€51) at the end of the first week of my working life. Even in 1981 this felt like a huge sum of money. Proudly, I handed it to my Ma on the Friday evening when I got home from work.

She handed it back to me saying: "You've earned it so you go and spend it."

The pride in our faces and hearts spoke more than any words could do.

My first assignment was to the Drugs Division in the Department. Now that might sound a little bit more glamorous than it actually was! As a Clerical Assistant, you were there to do the menial tasks of those above you, such as photocopying, filing and other general "dogs-body" work. But it gave me a grounding and I never felt that my disability impaired me from doing the work that other Clerical Assistants did. Perhaps the fact that I have competed successfully against my other able-bodied peers for promotion over the years proves that and, if I'm honest, has allowed me to feel a degree of pride in myself.

I felt, again for the first time in my life, that my father now looked at me as a man. Before this I had always thought that he looked at me rather guiltily, as if the difficulties I had in life were because of him – as if they reflected a flaw in his masculinity. I hasten to add that this never diluted his love for me. This love was neither verbally spoken nor physically expressed in any demonstrative way, yet I still knew that it was there. This was brought home to me a couple of years after his death. By way of background, my Da was a pretty handy footballer albeit with a bit of a fiery temperament. Definitely, the Wayne Rooney of his day! He was nicknamed "Dixie" after the famous England centre forward Dixie Dean. Anyway, I was going in to a shop in Ballyfermot when a man, whom I'd never met before, was coming out and said hello to me. I returned the greeting and he said: "You're Gerard aren't you, Dixie Maguire's son?"

I replied that I was, whereupon he said that he had been a good friend of my father's. He then said something that left me awestruck, proud, annoyed and in many ways so guilty.

"You know he was always talking about you. He was so proud of you."

I was flabbergasted. The man wished me well and went on his way. I was awestruck and proud that my Da felt like that about me, annoyed that in typical male fashion he would say these things to someone else and not to me, and guilty that I should have ever doubted that he felt that way about me.

As a child, I always felt that I had driven a wedge between my father and mother – that so much of my Ma's time was taken up with me that other parts of her life and marriage were neglected. Yet when I was a child it was to my Da that I turned when a question that had troubled me just had to be answered for my peace of mind.

"Because I have this disability, will I die sooner than someone who hadn't got it?" I asked him one night. I remember he was in bed reading when I asked him this.

He sat up in bed, startled that such a thing should be troubling my young mind. He picked his words of answer as carefully as if he'd been facing a High Court Judge: "I asked the doctors that question myself because I was worried, like you, and they told me that you would live as long as anyone else would. Your disability will have no bearing on this."

Neither of us showed any emotion, we were just dealing with plain facts. Yet the fact that he had asked the question caused two reactions in me. Firstly I now knew that I was not facing premature death (a hell of a worry for me as a young boy) and secondly, joy that my Da loved me so much that he had asked the question in the first place.

Looking back, my father's love for me was never in question – mine for him was another matter or perhaps more accurately my demonstration of my love for him. I was so wrapped up in love, devotion and dependence, with my mother, that as a child and young adult, I neglected to show him much affection, if any. I made it difficult for him to feel part of my life.

When I started work, our relationship moved on to a new dimension – it became a friendship. We became buddies and it felt so good. I really was only beginning to get to know him, yes to love him, when in December 1985, one week before Christmas all that changed. My father became weak while cycling to work. He went to see his GP who said that he would prepare a letter of referral for him to be seen in hospital to find out what was wrong. He asked that somebody call down to his surgery later that day to collect the letter.

I went down to the surgery that evening when I got home from work. I went in to my father's GP expecting just to be given the letter but instead I received the news that my Da was dying and would most likely be dead by New Year's Day.

The doctor's words were blunt and to the point: "Your father is very sick – I'll be surprised if he lasts 'til the New Year."

To say I was shocked is one hell of an understatement. I had suspected that my Da was not well as he had begun to take a lot of sick leave from work. It was something which I had never seen him do before. This tell-tale sign spoke volumes.

The doctor went on to tell me that my Da had prostate cancer which appeared to have spread. This was discovered in tests which he'd had six months previously, the results of which it later transpired, were never passed on to my father. So there he was going blindly on with his daily routines, as best he could, while this thing was eating away inside him. Incredibly, this included cycling to and from work everyday, a round trip journey of about six miles. Also, he worked a shift pattern with the late shift finishing at 11 o'clock at night or sometimes into the early hours of the morning if overtime was available. And, as if this wasn't bad enough, the work he did involved manually loading and unloading materials from the factory's production line. He had carried on doing all this for months not knowing, due to medical incompetence, that cancer was marauding its way through him.

The GP advised me to bring my father straight to hospital.

I drove the half-mile journey home from the surgery on Ballyfermot Road in a daze. In that short journey my mind was racing. Do I arrive home and announce what I had just been told? Do I call my Ma and Da aside individually and tell them? Do I just tell one and not the other? What in the name of Christ was I to do? I don't know whether I consciously made a decision or whether I just did nothing but I arrived home and said: "I have the letter Da, will we go?" I felt like a total shit for not being up-front with him. But just at that time, my mind was cabbaged. He deserved to have someone answer the questions, which he would surely have asked, and I knew that I was just not that person.

I remember driving him to St James's Hospital, on that dark, dank Monday evening, feeling almost as though I was bringing him to the gallows.

My mother was utterly unaware of how ill my father was. My head was in a complete whirl when I left him in the hospital that Monday evening. I wanted to tell the other three as soon as possible so I rang Anne in work and said I needed to speak to her. We met in Bowes Pub in Fleet Street and I told her the awful news. She was as disbelieving as I and we both agreed that Mammy should know the full story.

We went home together to try to break the dreadful news. The picture I have of that night is as vivid now as if it had happened five minutes ago. When we arrived Mammy was sitting at her customary position at the kitchen table, peeling potatoes. After I told her the awful news her reaction was a bit unexpected.

"Will you stop messing Gerard, what did they say? What's wrong with him?"

It took a few more attempts before she finally believed that this was not some sick joke. I watched as it began to sink in – that her husband, the man she had pledged to spend her days with, was about to be taken from her. They were both in their very early sixties.

The protector in her came quickly to the fore. She was adamant that my father was not to be told how ill he was. My Ma was utterly immovable on this.

She said that she would tell Dominic and Liam. It was now nearly 10 o'clock. I had left my father in the hospital at 6.30. Three and a half hours of madness had passed which had felt more like three and a half days – madness that I would have given anything to have not had to go through.

Anne and I went to see my father's consultant in St James's Hospital the following morning. We were terrified that my Da would see us as he would surely know that something was wrong if he saw us in the hospital so early in the morning. While we were waiting for the consultant near my Da's ward, we noticed my Da walking down the corridor. We immediately ducked into a room to avoid him seeing us. I remember thinking it was just totally surreal. I was sure someone was going to wake me up from the nightmare. It was Christmas week for God's sake. I kept saying to myself, this can't be happening.

But after meeting the consultant we were left in no doubt that this was happening – and happening at a very fast rate. He told us there was nothing they could do except to make whatever time my father had left as comfortable as possible. With the GP's words in my mind that my Da had only days to live, I asked the consultant what he meant by "the time left". He said it was impossible to say but that "it wouldn't be long".

I asked why the results of the tests which my father had had done some months back were not passed on to him, so that he could have been receiving treatment.

The Consultant was at a loss to explain why this had happened and in my innocence, naivety, downright greenness, I accepted that. To this day, I feel guilty that I didn't knock on every door of that hospital to find out why my father was neglected in this way. He would have done it for me and yet I didn't do it for him. I will take that guilt to my grave.

After some emergency treatment, my Da was allowed home a couple of days before Christmas – it would be our last Christmas together as a complete family.

What followed were months of utter sadness. Watching my father, who in many ways I'd newly found and who now, without any doubt was dearly loved by me, fading away tore me in two. So much of the next few months were spent either visiting him in hospital or watching over him at home.

In February 1986, Mammy and Daddy went to see the consultant who told my Da exactly what was wrong with him. The cancer which had originated in his prostate had now spread to his other organs. Ironically, because my Da was so fit, this had allowed the cancer to prosper. Basically it had fit and healthy cells to eat away at. Mammy said that Daddy's first question to her when he heard the news was: "Do the kids know?"

When Mammy said that we did, he said: "Thank God, because I don't know how I would be able to tell them."

The news about my father's condition quickly spread. I don't know whether it's an Irish thing but people love talking about and passing on bad news. One of our relatives (I won't be any more specific than that for reasons which will become apparent!) was a chronic hypochondriac. You name it, she had it. This used to always amuse my Da. One day I was at home with him when she arrived for a visit.

"God Willie," she said, "I've only just heard the bad news about your prostate. I know exactly how you're feeling because I've been having terrible trouble with my prostate lately."

My Da and I looked at one another. I thought that this might just be a bridge too far for him but he couldn't keep the laughter in. He said to me later that he didn't think that he'd ever laugh again so she did him more good than she'll ever know!

Despite their efforts, the medical team could not prevent him from suffering what must have been incredible pain. Hard as it may seem to believe, but, sadly in 1986, the science of Palliative Care was not as enlightened as it is now. I remember one evening I was in the bathroom and my Da obviously thought that he was alone upstairs. He was in my parents' bedroom crying lowly and pleading in a quiet voice: "Jesus please take this pain away."

I sat there, trying to keep quiet in case I embarrassed him at this time of utter vulnerability. At the same time I was so desperate to reach out to him, to protect him and tell him that I was there. But I sat there and the time passed.

In his final stay in hospital in August 1986, he began
to see in his mind, or maybe even with his eyes, his mother
who had died many years before any of us were born.
He was devoted to his mother and apparently was deeply
affected by her death at a young age. One day when I
visited him he told me that only two women came in to
see him in hospital,

"Who?" I asked.

"Your Ma and my Ma," he answered.

I began to panic, thinking that his mind was going.
However, I can see now that in fact it was his spirit which
was preparing to leave this world, being claimed back by
his mother.

On the night of Wednesday, August 13, I went to the
hospital to see him. We were alone and he begged me,
with tears in his eyes, to bring him home. I tried as best as
I could to pacify him, saying that he was in the best place
to be looked after. I said that it was a horrible, windy, wet
night, which it was, and that I just couldn't. He begged me
all the more, so much so that I just had to leave.

I got outside the ward and sank to the floor,
inconsolable. Was I doing right leaving him there? Should
I just gather his stuff together and bring him out of there,
since plainly there was nothing more that they could do
for him? Here I was, 23 years old, greener than grass, with
the ability to make my father happy and I was letting him
down – letting him down in a way that I knew that he
would never let me down.

The hospital rang at 6 o'clock the following morning
to say that my Da was extremely agitated and was insisting
that he be brought home. I drove there with my Ma at
breakneck speed, while Liam followed behind us, going

through many red lights, to get to him. I knew that I was doing something which I should have done the previous evening, thus saving my father an unnecessary night of stress and anxiety.

A few months previously, an uninsured driver had crashed into me on my way home from work. He left my driver's side door fairly bashed up. At that time, to claim on my insurance would have screwed up my no-claims bonus. This and the fact that I couldn't claim off the other guy's insurance, meant that the door remained unfixed. When we got my father ready to come home, and Liam and me were trying to get him into the car, he refused to get in. He insisted on going around to the side where the dent was, to see it for himself. He wanted to make sure that it was my car that he was getting into and that we weren't bringing him anywhere else but home.

My heart bled for him.

As we were driving past Downey's pub on Ballyfermot Road, his local, I said to him: "I bet you wouldn't mind sneaking in there for a quick pint now Da, would you?"

And he said: "No son, I just want to go home to be with you all."

The significance of the damaged car was further re-enforced some months later after my father died. I used go to his grave every day as the pain of his loss, my guilt and other confused emotions ran riot. One day I went up to visit the grave during my lunchtime from work. I had bought a new car a few weeks previously, trading the other car in without ever having it repaired. When I pulled in to the cemetery car park, there wasn't another car there. After visiting the grave, I came back to the car park and there were now two cars there, mine and another one parked right beside it. To my amazement I saw that the other car was the one which I had driven my father home from the hospital in, those few months previously. The dent was gone, but the memories came flooding back. A shiver went through me and then I began to see that maybe this was a sign from my Da. He was telling me that there was no need to visit the grave every day, that I did not need to torment myself and that guilt and regrets were unnecessary.

We brought my Da home on Thursday, August 14. I don't know whether the cancer had poisoned him so much or if it was the medication he was on, perhaps it was a combination of both, but he was so confused. He was almost childlike in his words. Again, seeing this was so distressing. In one of his last lucid moments, he called me over to his bedside and whispered to me: "I want you to do me a big favour Ger. I have some money hidden under the carpet in the front room upstairs. I want you to look after your Mammy with it."

This was the first time that he had spoken aloud that he knew his time was nearing the end. His desire to get home from hospital was an unspoken admission he knew he was dying and now this, the first verbal one. Here I was, the person whom I always thought my Da would never be able to depend upon to do anything meaningful for him, being entrusted by him to care for the one thing he cared for more than anything else, my Ma. At that time of horror, I felt so proud and honoured. As I sat in their room for some reason I thought of a time when I was a teenager and he had bought her a box of chocolates as he always used to do if they had had a tiff and bridges needed mending. After he gave her the chocolates I remember he whispered to me: "She's an awful woman, I'm always the one who makes up! But God I worship the ground she walks on".

I went upstairs to his hiding-place and found IR£100 (€127). When I came down, I showed him that I had found it.

He said: "I know it's not a lot, just promise me you'll look after her."

I told him that I would. It is a promise that I hope I kept.

On August 22, 1986 at 6.15 pm, on a wet Friday evening, as I held his hand in a bed specially arranged for him downstairs in our house, my father died. During the final week of his life, I washed him, shaved him, gave him his medication and tried as best I could to make his last days as comfortable as possible.

At one stage, we asked him if he would like a pint of Guinness, his favourite tipple. He nodded eagerly, unable now to speak. Various people tried to give the drink to him, holding him up in the bed, with the glass to his mouth. He consistently refused to drink and kept nodding towards me.

In the end I sat on his bed and held him in my arms. His muscular, supremely fit frame, maintained by my Da religiously doing 25 press-ups every morning before going to work, was now gone, eroded by that awful disease. He felt tiny in my embrace. I held the pint to his lips. He drank it and you could see that he was savouring every drop. I heard his youngest sister, my Auntie Maureen, say: "Look, he wanted Gerard to give it to him."

My heart almost burst with pride.

Shortly after coming home from hospital, my father had had a catheter attached which was filling less and less each day, as his body slowly shut down. About an hour after drinking the Guinness, the catheter bag filled up for the first time in days. My mother was delighted at what she saw as a positive development and asked me to ring the hospital to see what this meant. I knew in my heart that this didn't mean anything positive but she was desperate and insisted that I ring.

She sat on the stairs in front of me while I talked to one of the team who had been treating my Da. The doctor assured me that this was normal and didn't mean anything. When I told Mammy what the doctor had said she then asked: "So does this mean that he's getting better?"

My heart broke for her. She was so desperate for anything to cling on to, any sliver of hope that her man was going to stay with her.

"No Ma it doesn't," I told her. "He's still going to die."

Even her optimism was short-lived, as the decline in him over the next few days was startling.

My father was buried on the morning of Monday, August 25, 1986. It was in the middle of Hurricane Charlie which caused so much destruction throughout the country. The Parish Priest, Father Supple, said to me in the graveyard after my father had been laid to rest: "Take your mother home and look after her."

The family started to go their separate ways after my Da's death. Anne had married a few months before he died and Dominic and Liam married their respective 'Marys' in the months afterwards. So the house which had always seemed so full, with voices reverberating through it changed quickly and dramatically. It's often said that the grief of losing a loved one only hits when all the fuss surrounding the funeral has gone, when relatives and friends return to their own lives. Our house after my father's death now comprised of Mammy, our Golden Labrador Ben, and me. It really was always ever going to be thus. If she thought that she could put her feet up and have me mind her for a change, however, then events over the next few years would significantly change her way of thinking.

The first Christmas without my Da was surreal in many ways. I remember standing at his grave on that first Christmas morning after he died. Myself and Mammy stood there, vacantly staring at the recently erected headstone bearing his name and at his smiling photograph. I remember her looking at me and she just sobbed.

Somehow as a family we got through the rest of the day. But the inescapable fact that our family, for the very first Christmas, was short of one hugely important person and this did cast a massive shadow on the day.

Less than two weeks after that first Christmas without my Da, Anne gave birth to her first child, Ciarán. He would have been my father's first grandchild. Anne had been pregnant at the time of his death. She had such a rough time during her pregnancy, both from a health aspect and also because of our Da's cancer. She had to try to deal with the knowledge that her father, whom she loved so dearly, was so gravely ill and then cope with his subsequent death. The birth itself proved to be difficult and Mammy was so worried about her. When she received the phone call in the early hours of Sunday, January 4, 1987, that her first grandchild was born and Anne, having gone through such a tough time, was alright, she was so relieved – all of us were. We had some relatives staying with us from England at the time so there was a great fuss made of the arrival of her first grandchild.

In the middle of all the hullabaloo I noticed that Mammy wasn't in the room with us. I went upstairs to see if she was alright and I heard her crying in her room. I knew, as she did, how overjoyed and proud my Da would have been if he had lived to see this day and I knew that this realisation was really being felt by my Ma. This realisation that he just wasn't here with her to share their joy.

It set off a chain reaction of negative thoughts in me. In typically self-indulgent fashion, I began to wonder had I taken too much of her time, time that she could and should have spent with my father, her husband. I knew that it was time that she could not now spend with him, time that she could never claim back. This tendency to self-analysis, to almost self-torture, was about to become a regular visitor in my head – a visitor who was about to make my life, and by extension my Ma's life, unbearable.

FIVE

UNDER ATTACK

Over the next few years, myself and my Ma got used to the difference which had taken place in our lives. Mammy worked three nights a week in the local bingo hall, went to daily morning mass with her friends and, for the first time in my recollection, she actually seemed to be living and enjoying life for herself, rather than for someone else. One by one, her eight grandchildren arrived and she gloried in them all.

I knew as each one of them was born that she would have given anything for my father to have been there to share her joy. And equally it must have been so hard on Anne and Liam, as their respective children came into the world that their kids' grandfather wasn't there to see them.

I continued my career in the Civil Service, enjoying

promotions along the way which, I know, made my Ma incredibly proud. As unassuming as she was she did tell anyone who would listen about her Gerard's promotions! Many times neighbours would congratulate me and as I hadn't said anything it was obvious where they had gotten their information from! The fact that I had made her proud after all her struggles with me chuffed me beyond words. These were my medals to show her that her work had not been in vain.

We lived incredibly happily together – two separate lives, yet intertwined with all that had gone before.

In 1994, however, my world shook with the most serious jolt. I had felt for some time that my mother was not looking well. She looked tired and much paler than normal. My worst fears were realised when one Sunday in April that year, while her brother Tommy was home on a visit from England, my mother suffered a heart attack at home.

I had been out and about that morning. As per normal, I would have expected to arrive back to the aroma of Sunday dinner on the go. When I got back, the absence of that familiar smell was the first thing that I noticed. Tommy said that Mammy had not felt well when she came home from Mass and had gone up to bed. This was so out of character for her but the irrational thought processes you go through at times like that are incredible. I remember thinking if I rushed upstairs, as fast as I could, it would make the immediacy of the situation all the more real. If I went about normally, doing a few things around the house, however, and then went up to see her it would feel like business as usual. But I knew this was ridiculous. So I went upstairs half-expecting, fully praying, that she would be sitting up in bed, maybe even listening to the radio. But no, instead she was lying down in obvious discomfort. She didn't want to speak, never mind move. I had seen my Ma with colds and flus over the years which would have floored most of us and she would battle through as if there was absolutely nothing wrong with her. But this was a completely different scenario.

In shock, I asked her if she wanted me to call a doctor, her immediate acceptance was, again, uncharacteristic. With hindsight, I should have just made a decision and rang for an ambulance immediately.

The doctor arrived at about two o'clock and said that she felt that Mammy should go to hospital without delay. She said that she had already called for an ambulance.

My heart was racing. Despite my best efforts to stay calm, I knew that a doctor would not ring for an ambulance unless something was seriously amiss.

I was terrified. Seeing her being brought down the stairs on a stretcher and being put in an ambulance brought all sorts of potential horror scenarios into my head. For the first time in my life, the thought of losing her became a very real possibility and I wondered if I would be able to cope without her – not physically but mentally.

I was standing at the bottom of the stairs when the ambulance men brought her down.

"Don't worry Ger, I'll be grand," she said to me.

A panoply of potential horrors flashed through my mind in that instant.

Thankfully, as heart attacks go, it was a mild one but it was a serious shot across the bows, both for her and for me.

She was in hospital for a little over a week. The fears

which I felt seeing my Ma so sick and vulnerable were
equally shared by the other three. We were just not used
to seeing her ill. Okay, a cold or some other bug now and
then, but nothing which literally felled her, as this had
done. I knew how lost I would be if anything happened
to her and I knew that my brothers and sister were having
exactly the same thoughts and exactly the same fears.

The hospital wanted her to spend some time in
a convalescent home and they made the mistake of
suggesting this to her. She was having none of it. When
I went into the hospital to see her that day she made me
promise that this would not happen. She wanted my word
that I would bring her home. Again I was startled at her
reaction and by her vulnerability. Here was someone who
I had relied on for so much in my life, and she was now
pleading with me to bring her home.

And so I did. I know that the hospital staff thought that
I was wrong but I knew in my heart that I was right.

Such a bolt from the blue as a parent suffering a heart
attack cannot help but affect every member of the family.
And we were no different. All our fears were founded on
this sudden exposure of our beloved mother's mortality.
When Mammy had her heart attack that Sunday, while
she was receiving emergency treatment, we walked around
the hospital like dazed children. For that's what you revert
to, no matter how old you are, when a parent becomes
vulnerable through illness – you become a child all over
again.

I became tiresomely, and I'm sure annoyingly,
overprotective of her after her heart attack. The very real
possibility of life without my Ma had been brought home
to me and I don't mind admitting that I didn't like it one

little bit.

Not long after that scare, she developed Age Related Macular Degeneration. This is a horrible condition which can happen so quickly. In simple terms, the retina is a very important part of your eye. The macula is at the very centre of the retina and basically controls your ability to see. If the macula begins to malfunction or die away then you're basically in trouble. And that's exactly what happened to my mother and, from what I can remember, it happened very quickly and without much warning. Her eyesight deteriorated so quickly and so dramatically. In no time at all she struggled to see a few feet in front of her. Doctors assured her that she would never go completely blind but unfortunately her eyesight would never improve either. As the name of the condition also suggests, they told her it would degenerate. She had surgery to remove cataracts but this made no improvement at all. I was convinced, and remain so, that she'd had an event, a stroke perhaps, when she had her heart attack. I think it precipitated this terrible decline in her eyesight. Despite voicing my many concerns to doctors on this and their reluctance to commit to this theory, I still firmly hold to that view.

For someone whose life was suddenly completely changed by this sudden loss of sight, she tried her best to carry on as normally as she could. She had loved to read newspapers and books and to look at TV (especially 'Eastenders' and snooker!) and in fairness for a while she did manage to still watch television. She'd be sitting with her nose almost pressing the screen until it either became pointless or soul-destroying for her to do so.

I used to read the newspaper aloud for her or if she had heard something on the radio news which interested her she would get me to read the newspaper report of it. It may not be every single man's idea of having a good time but I used to absolutely love it. It kept her involved with the interesting news of the day and it made me feel as if I was doing something practically useful to help her, as she had done for me on countless occasions before. All the family bought her audio books, which she enjoyed, but she always said that she preferred when I read books to her! Maybe it was the budding thespian in me which gave her a laugh but I got a great kick out of it.

I knew, however, that behind all this putting a brave face on, she was so frustrated. I was so angry at the injustice of it. Where was the justice in someone who had spent her life so selflessly and who would help anyone in need, being afflicted in such a cruel and horrible way? Where was the God that she had shown such devotion to, despite all the adversities that He had visited upon her?

But as much as I questioned how a loving God could, as I saw it, betray one of his most loyal servants, she never once did. She truly believed that it was His will that had brought about this condition in her and who was she to question that. It was, in a strange way, so inspiring to behold and just made me love her all the more, if that was possible.

When I was not at home, I worried that she would be okay by herself. When she was out, again I worried about her. It was an unhealthy existence for both of us. The family were always calling in but, in fairness, they had their own lives to lead. I know it is perfectly natural to worry about someone you love at appropriate times, but to live your life, as I was, in a constant state of anxiety, can be so wearing.

I sought solace in alcohol. It was at home obviously, as I was not able to go out without being worried sick about her being alone at home. I drank when Mammy went to bed. It was almost as if I was trying to cover up the unhappiness and frustration which now pervaded both of our lives. I knew well what I was trying to do because I remember logically and consciously thinking it out at the time. I was trying to drink myself into an early grave so that I would die before her, as the thought of having to live my life without her was too unbearable to contemplate. And I also reckoned that if I anaesthetised myself enough with alcohol then I might be able to chill out and not let my feelings about my disability consume so much of my head space.

I am not, in any way, blaming my mother for what became my dependence on drink. She was utterly, utterly blameless and to suggest otherwise would be to sully her memory which I would never allow anyone to do. There was one person and one person alone responsible for my dependence and that was me. It was my inability to cope with my disability and the huge limitations that it placed, and places, upon me. My Ma never led me to believe that she knew – maybe she did and chose to ignore it. I think it would be wrong to speculate.

Very quickly, as my dependence on drink grew, I was drinking an average of four bottles of vodka a week. I used to stock up at the weekend, buying a bottle in different off-licences. I mainly shopped on the north side of Dublin where I reckoned there was little hope of anyone I knew meeting me and seeing my stockpile. I used to feel so shitty sneaking the bottles past my Ma and then sneaking the empties out. I just felt horrible, like some sort of sleaze. I had never deceived her and yet here I was, I thought, living a life of deception and, if I'm honest, selfishness.

Quickly, rapidly in fact, I was no longer taking the drink. In no time at all the drink had well and truly taken me. I was obsessed with ensuring that I had my full quota for the week stored up. It had a vice-like grip on me. The first few drinks had the effect that sensible drinking should have on you – they made me feel happy. For a time, my misery about my disability was blocked out. But, before long, that sense of 'happiness' wore down. Then the realisation hit that no matter how much I drank to drown away my disability, I could only in truth submerge it for a time. It was always going to re-surface. And then naturally came the guilt – the guilt of deception, of deceiving my mother, which left me despising myself even more than I already did, of deceiving my family and, ultimately, deceiving myself. This guilt and the helplessness that I soon felt in its powers made me feel like shit. I found out how apt the alcoholics' saying 'First the man takes the drink, then the drink takes the drink, then the drink takes the man', really is.

My feelings of self-consciousness, at that time, were beginning to wear me down. I was so tired of my disability and despised it intensely. I saw friends and family getting married and having children and I longed for the happiness which I knew that would have brought me, if only I was in their place. Let me try to explain – my disability had always been a drawback in the love stakes. This is not because I hadn't tried – I had. Virtually all my attempts ended in the "let's just be friends" line. For years I'd had an intense craving to be a parent, yet I knew that my disability was always going to be a serious impediment to any relationship either beginning or developing. This is not a reflection on either the respective girls or on me – it is just an experiential fact. For instance, ask yourself a question – could you spend your life with a seriously disabled person no matter how interesting or charming or funny or whatever positive characteristic they may have? If I had the option I'm not sure that I could. With all this in mind I felt that my role was pre-defined – my life was caring for my mother and trying to drown out the negative thoughts which kept knocking at the door of my head. Looking back, I realise that not alone was I drowning myself in alcohol but I was also immersing myself in feelings of self-pity and self-loathing.

The manifestations of all these negativities came to a head in 1998 when I began to suffer from the most appalling panic attacks. The term "Panic Attack" is bandied about, almost as a sexy euphemism, by people who may suffer the occasional bout of nervousness, or who might shy away from public occasions. Believe me, panic attacks are events which can grind your life to a complete halt. In their embryonic state, they can be just those symptoms of nervousness which, if left unchecked, become multiplied firstly tenfold, then a hundredfold, and so on, until they are completely out of control and have taken over your life.

My panic attacks started exactly like that. Initially, they began as slight anxieties – the little knot in the stomach when you were going somewhere new or doing something different. Very soon, and without any warning, this nervous tension, which in some cases can be turned into a positive and help to focus the mind, instead turned colossally negative. They became a threat to my life, as more and more I struggled to cope with the huge pressure that this panic was building up inside my head. I often thought during the worst phases of my panic attacks that I would rather have ten physical disabilities than the psychological one which I had now acquired. I remember at the height of the panic attacks visiting my favourite church on God's Earth, in Chapelizod, and sitting there, in the empty church, calling God all the names under the Sun. I was using profanities which should never be used on a street corner never mind in a Church, because I was so angry with God for giving me this "second" disability.

I can't be sure exactly how and when the panic attacks actually started. At their peak, they caused me to shake so violently that I felt as if I was having some sort of fit or seizure. I particularly remember one morning when I was driving into work. I was stopped at traffic lights at the Ha'penny Bridge when an attack gripped me. I began to shake uncontrollably and could see that people passing in front of my car were looking in at me. I'm sure they were wondering just what the hell was wrong with me. Deep in my heart, I knew what was causing these panic attacks – my hatred of my disability and ergo of myself. I was fed up with feeling that everyone watched me as I walked in a different way to the way they walked. I was sick of my ever increasing feelings of utter inferiority. Being in public places became a complete nightmare, especially going to work. Some mornings I would sit in the car in the car park in work unable, through fear, to get out. And then, more often than not, I would finally leave the car, get just inside the front door of the building and come to a complete standstill. I was unable to walk forwards towards the lift or back towards my car. Such times, which might last for a matter of seconds or up to ten minutes, were unspeakably lonely moments trapped in an irrational state of suspended animation, unable to ask for help and yet terrified that someone might offer me help. On many occasions I used the service entrance to the building. It was significantly further away than the front door but meant that I could come and go with fewer people seeing me.

One particular evening, I was going home but to my dismay the side service door was closed which meant that I had to use the front door. Less than three yards from the door, I suddenly, without warning, found myself grinding to a halt. I stood there, frozen with terror, the sanctuary of my car visible to me, no more than 20 feet away. I stood in that position for about half an hour. Many people asked me if I was alright and I replied that I was waiting on someone. I longed to have the courage to say to each person that asked: "Please, please help me."

I tried to move my feet so many times during that half hour period but without success. It was as if the connection between my brain and my legs had been severed. How I eventually got to my car that evening, I'm not exactly sure. But it left such an indelible mark on me. I feared a repetition everyday afterwards, which merely accentuated my panic.

The fear and sometimes the anticipation of having a similar panic attack quickly spread to every other area of my life – shopping, socialising and even going to church. You name it – nowhere was safe. Two contrasting experiences show the scatter-gun effect panic attacks can have on your life. I was at an anniversary Mass for my father in our local church. I had never experienced a panic attack in a church before. Maybe on some level I had taken solace in the thought that surely I was safe in God's house. When the Mass was over, all my family got up to leave. I tried to go as well but quickly recognised the symptoms – panic, fear, paralysis. My family all wondered why I sat back down. I said I would follow them out after saying a few prayers.

As I sat there a local charismatic prayer group were preparing to have their weekly meeting in the church. Many of them looked at me and I assume thought that I was a new member of the group. I sat in my seat for an hour, transfixed not by thoughts of solemnity but of how, and more importantly, when, and even more crucially, if, this panic was going to lift and allow me to go home to join the rest of my family. When I eventually did leave the church and got home, everyone asked me where I'd been. I was so ashamed of myself I couldn't tell them the truth about what had happened and made something up, anything to deflect from having to tell the truth.

I have a funny feeling that this may have been the incident which triggered a sense of suspicion in my mother. She was incredibly intuitive about me, which was hardly surprising given the time and energy she had expended on raising me. In a way, I knew from her facial expression when I got home that she thought something wasn't right but she didn't say anything. Perhaps she didn't know how to broach the subject. If she had suspicions about the drinking perhaps she felt the same way about that. Maybe she took a "least said soonest mended approach". More likely, if I'm honest, was that she was concerned that if she voiced aloud her fears then instead of acting positively to rectify it, I would use her knowledge of yet another flaw in me as another stick to beat myself with. In any event,

I'm sure, not for the first time, that I caused her worry and anxiety and I am deeply sorry for that.

The second incident happened one afternoon as I was coming out of a shop with my obligatory bottle of vodka in hand. I was tantalisingly close to my car, when again I ground to a standstill, unable to move another centimetre. Feeling so self-conscious outside an off-licence, in the middle of the afternoon, with a bottle in a brown paper bag in my hand, I tried to physically do what my mind was refusing to allow me to do, walk. The two key components railed against one another and against my efforts to move, and I fell to the ground. The bottle of vodka smashed around me and I was left literally sitting in its contents. A sense of degradation, loneliness and every other negative feeling you can imagine, enveloped me. I literally crawled back on all fours to my car. My hands were bleeding from the glass and my jeans were soaked by the vodka as I sped away to a quiet place where I could weep in peace.

Throughout all this mental horror, a dear and close friend of mine was the only person I spoke to about how I felt and what affect all this was having on me. His words of encouragement helped me so much – he knows who he is, and in case I never did before, I thank him from the bottom of my heart now, for all his help.

These two instances had such a debilitating effect on me. It also exposed that I was vulnerable to an attack anywhere. There was no safe haven. As awful as these, among many other, experiences were, they did make me realise that this problem was now far too big for me to handle alone. I knew I had to make some changes.

I had decided to job share in work on a week-on, week-off, basis. I did this, genuinely, for two reasons.

Firstly, I began to feel that with my mother's increasingly failing sight, it was time that I gave back to her what she had always given to me in abundance – care, time and attention. Secondly, it was a chance for me to seek refuge from the panic, to be safe at home, sheltered away from the outside world. I knew that this was a dangerous path, though, as I was sure that this could be the precursor to a time when I was neither able, nor would I want to, leave the house. From what I have read many people who have developed the curse of panic attacks describe how in the end the panic has driven them into becoming chronic agoraphobics. The panic simply became so dominant that it was much easier just to stay at home. I could see that you could retreat into that sanctuary until you had retreated so far back that it is virtually impossible for you to move forward. And while home was my place of safety, I wasn't happy becoming a prisoner in it. And I also had Mammy to consider – and she was always, in my mind, much more important to me than I was to myself. Even saying this, I knew that I was going deeper and deeper into my psychological morass. If I allowed this to continue I was afraid that the time would come when I would be more of a hindrance than a help to my mother. I knew I needed professional help.

Once I had reached that decision I was determined that if this was to work I would have to be honest with my mother. I could not have started the journey of recuperation without her knowledge and hopefully her support. I chose the timing of telling her deliberately. Sunday afternoon was one of the few joys in my life at that time. Myself and my Ma would be cooking the dinner together, sitting down to eat, just the two of us, talking about anything and everything. And it was on such a Sunday that I told her exactly how my mind was feeling and how panic was such a strong, and increasingly overpowering, element in my life.

She confirmed my suspicions that she had felt I was in trouble when she told me that she'd known there was something wrong. Why should I have been surprised when she knew me so well? She said that no matter how much help I needed to get things right, either financially or in terms of moral support, I was to promise her that I believed that she could and would provide it.

I sobbed telling her. I felt as if I had betrayed her. I felt that all the work that she had put into the physical side of my life had been negated by the psychological demons which I had allowed in.

In a stoic way, unemotionally and incredibly practically, she told me that no matter who or where I went for help, she would be there for me.

I told her I was ashamed of myself. Looking back, I was so wrong to use those words because I'm sure it hurt her to hear me say such things about myself, particularly after all that she had done, not to mention all that she had sacrificed for me. However, I was determined to be as honest as possible.

I don't believe she ever broke the confidences we shared that day. Without her help, this time carrying me in her heart instead of in her arms, as she'd done over 35 years previously, I would not have survived the months to come.

Six

Reaching Out for Help

After that Sunday, the sense of relief I felt having told Mammy what was happening was incredible. Never was the phrase "a problem shared is a problem halved" more apposite. And I knew because it was Mammy whom I had shared the problem with and she had dealt with it in exactly the way that I would have wanted her to, all just seemed to bring a light into what was a very bleak time. It also made it real – I could no longer run away from the problem. Once I had told Mammy about it, I knew that she would not allow me to drag this on any further. I had promised her that I would seek help without delay and I didn't want to break that promise.

With this in mind, the following day, I drove to the Phoenix Park, to the Papal Cross, to be precise. I prayed for the strength to make the phone call to someone who might help me. I had not done the research which you really should do when looking for such help. I was that desperate that I rang the first counselling service I saw in the Golden Pages. I rang the number on my mobile phone and to my relief an answering machine came on. A man's voice explained that he was most likely in session with someone but asking that you leave your name and number and he would get back to you. In typical coward's fashion, I was about to hang up without doing so, stupidly consoling myself with the knowledge that I had tried to seek help, when the message ended with him saying: "Please do leave your details, you obviously rang looking for help – I will help you."

On hearing those words, without hesitation I left my name and number.

The counsellor, Frank, rang me back within half an hour and after a little persuasion on his part, we arranged to meet on the following Thursday evening. Of course the usual questions about whether his office was disabled-friendly or not reared their head. Even at this precarious time in my life, I still had to fret about such things. No wonder I was so messed up. I thought his office was probably anything but user-friendly for me but suddenly I didn't care. If it meant me crawling up or down stairs (which I subsequently sometimes had to do) then I was determined to just do it. I had got such a vibe of optimism from Frank on the phone that I was determined to carry this through.

When I got home, I told my Ma that I had arranged the appointment. Looking back now I am in awe at her reaction and how insightful she was. A woman of her generation might be excused for scoffing at the notion of seeking help through a counsellor, maybe instead using the "Pull yourself together – you've little to be worrying you" approach. What a disservice I paid her. She viewed this man, whom she had never met, nor ever would meet, as the person who was going to bring me back from the edge.

The next few days were nervously spent with my many thoughts of just what on earth was I going to do if Frank couldn't help me. I left so early for my 6 o'clock appointment on that boiling hot Thursday in early June that I arrived way before time. I passed the minutes sitting in the car park of Our Lady of Good Shepherd Church in Churchtown, praying and praying that this was the beginning of the end of the nightmare that I was living.

When I went in to see Frank, I could hardly speak as I was hyperventilating. At times I was even unable to get enough air into my lungs to allow me to speak aloud. I eventually composed myself, and, after a few preliminaries, I explained how I hated myself, my disability, the many restrictions which it had placed on me during my life and the terrible mental torture that it appeared to be bringing me now. I explained that I knew I was always going to be disabled. I wasn't sure if I was ever going to be able to accept that or, in fact, wanted to, for that matter. I just wanted to feel less inadequate, to not feel as if I was worthless in other people's eyes, to like myself basically. This was the first time that I had voiced all these fears aloud and here I was doing it with a total stranger. When I got down in the past, poor Mammy used to have to put up with my moaning! She always knew what to say to get me through such times. But for all her many abilities, this was just too big for her. For once, she knew that I needed more than her words of encouragement and I think that she was sad about that.

In fairness, Frank explained that I was the first disabled client he'd ever had so the journey we were about to start would be an education for both of us. To begin with, Frank made me realise that it was important to recognise the magnitude of the effect which my disability had, and would continue to have, on my life. I had moved from a grudging acceptance of it to a downright hatred of it. It would be utterly pointless to try to get me to love my disability – my anger and negative feelings were legitimate feelings to have towards something which had had such a devastating impact on my life. But I did have to come to an acceptance that I would have to find a place for it in my life.

In essence, Frank explained that if I looked at my mind as a computer, what was happening was that the programmes which I had lived with all my life had now become confused. They had, in effect, been attacked by a virus. When a computer is attacked by a virus it needs to be re-programmed and in a way that's what my mind needed. He would help me do this by talking, by teasing things out and by hypnotherapy as well. He would help me until I felt that panic was no longer a visitor who would find a welcome home in my head. Our aim was to get to the point where I would treat it as an unruly guest, who had been banned forever. Frank said that after my first session of hypnotherapy and counselling, when I left his office I would be filled with a sense of exhilaration. I remember thinking how much of an aspiration that was – exhilaration was not something I experienced much, if ever, in my life. But that evening I most certainly did feel exhilarated. I floated back to my car and felt so happy on the drive home. It was a feeling that no artificial substance ever invented could replicate. Christ, if I could bottle this feeling, I thought, I'd never need to look at a bottle of vodka again. And we hadn't even started the hypnotherapy yet!

Without prompting from anyone, I decided that it would be disingenuous of me to be going through this without telling Dominic, Anne and Liam. I didn't expect them to be active participants in my recovery – that was mainly down to me, I knew. I just felt that they should know but in a bizarre way, I was so nervous telling them. Not because they might think any less of me – I was sure they wouldn't. I was afraid that if I was in any way ham-fisted in my way of telling them that they just may not grasp the severity of the situation and the undoubted peril that I knew I was in. So individually, I told them.

Their reactions left me in no doubt that they fully comprehended the severity of the situation. Indeed, the very act of my telling them perhaps heightened their acknowledgement of what I was going through. Again, in typical fashion they were so supportive to me. When I asked them not to tell anyone else about it, they didn't ask me why. They simply agreed.

I knew why I wanted it kept quiet. I was ashamed of myself. Looking back it was an irrational emotion to feel but rationality was a total stranger to me at that time.

And so, for the next five months I went through weekly sessions with Frank. His task, he said, was to fill me with hope and reassurance. It was my first experience of hypnotherapy. I half-expected it to be done with him waving an old watch chain in front of me and saying "You're getting sleepier and sleepier". But I think I must have been watching too many Woody Allen movies! Instead Frank got me to relax through breathing techniques and as I did so he gradually and gently spoke of how relaxed I was becoming and how at peace I was feeling. So while you felt as if you were wide awake and aware of what was going on, you definitely were switched to a calmer place. The hour long session would race by while I was in that state of complete relaxation.

And while in that hypnotic state, Frank spoke words which made me realise that I was valued by others and that I should therefore value myself. He said time and time again that panic attacks would be a thing of the past soon. He said that the main task was not to get me to like my disability, as to try to do so would be patronising and pointless. He simply wanted me to reach a point where I had come to terms with the limitations that it placed upon me and to accept that these limitations were never going to go away but that I might find some way around the frustration I felt at them.

I have to be honest, I was so gripped by panic that I thought that these might have been empty promises on his behalf. Did he really know or appreciate how bad I was? And yet as the weeks went by, the need to sneak in and out through the side door in work dissipated. If I went into a packed church, I was slowly losing the need to sit in the first available seat. In fact I was beginning to walk up to the very front and sit there. In shopping centres, I no longer went there first thing in the morning when I knew it would be quiet – I went in the middle of the day when it was full. If I was invited somewhere where I really didn't want to go, I said no for that reason rather than the real reason for my many refusals lately – that I was scared bloody shitless.

There was the odd occasion when my disability kept rearing its ugly head and reminding me that it hadn't been beaten in this mental tug of war. There was the odd stumble or fall here, the odd turning up at a place I wanted to go to only to find it inaccessible, there. But I knew that I no longer needed the sanctuary of home. My life wasn't as exciting as I would have liked but it was what it was and now I could at least tackle it mentally, if not physically.

When I got home after each session, Mammy would ask me a million and one questions about how it had gone. She was so eager to be a part of my recovery. I don't think she ever really realised just how much a part of that recovery she was to be and like a fool I never ever told her. How I wish now that I had. After one session she asked me if she could go with me to the next one. I explained that this wasn't really possible as it was one-to-one counselling.

"No, I don't want to go in," she said. "I won't even get out of the car. I'd just like to go with you."

Such a simple, genuine gesture but one that spoke volumes of her determination to never let me go through any trying time alone.

Much as I would have loved for her to go with me, I decided not to be selfish. As there was no waiting room it would have meant her sitting by herself in the car for over an hour. There was no way I was putting her through that, even though I knew that she would have sat by herself in a car for the whole day if it was for me.

When I finished my months of sessions with Frank, Mammy could not have been happier if I had been cured of a serious illness. And yet in hindsight, that is exactly what I had – a serious illness. Too often, if the illness is not visible, we ignore it. Graveyards are full of people who were too afraid to acknowledge the mental tortures which life had thrown at them. Too often those graves are filled by people who have chosen to end their own lives. I know, without a single shadow of doubt, that had I not sought and received such expert help I would have chosen that path. It is not cowardice – a foolish charge levelled at people who end their lives. It's just an overwhelming tiredness and mental exhaustion that sleep can't salve. It's not selfish either. In such troubled eyes it can almost be viewed as selfless. The feeling is that you are too much of a burden on those who love you – that this is the best way you can see in reciprocating that love. I think that is why we should remove expressions like "commit suicide" – commit has such negative, illegal connotations. I am in no way advocating anyone to end their life. If there was no other option perhaps… but I found that there were options. Exhaust those options. Cling on to the faintest of lights in the darkness of your mental gloom. Seek help in making that light burn brighter. It is not an easy or a short journey. But it is a journey worth undertaking.

I was blessed that I had a mother, a family and a good friend who saw me through those dismal days. And God they were dismal days. Without that help and support, I would truly have been lost. My heart goes out to the many who are not as fortunate and who feel compelled to seek a permanent solution to what, with the kind of help that I got, should only be a temporary problem.

Throughout my sessions with Frank, I deliberately didn't explore the increasingly dependent effect that drink was having in my life. This was because I didn't want to stop drinking – in any event I was certain that I wouldn't have been able to. It was my pressure valve release. But I was fooling myself. I knew that my health was suffering and that if I didn't stop soon I was going to die. I was beginning to wake up during the night with terrible pains from my gut and liver areas. I didn't need a doctor to confirm for me what was causing this. I was terrified that Mammy would get up out of bed one morning and find me dead. I could have died from having fallen or from choking on my vomit or because my liver had burst from the pummelling I was giving it. I just could not do that to her. But I knew that drink had such a grip on me.

There was one hope, however. Drink no longer gave me the enjoyment, the escape that it once did. It did not give me any buzz now. Instead the hold it had over me filled me with revulsion. I realised that for so long I had viewed it as a close friend whereas now it had become my sworn enemy. It had become almost functionary, like taking a dreaded prescribed medication.

The decision to stop was taken on December 7, 2000. I had driven my Ma, her brother Dave and his wife Hannah, to an old folks' Christmas dinner at a football club about two miles away. It was a filthy night, with wind and rain lashing down. I told them I would be back to collect them at 1.00 am. When I arrived, I could see my Ma clinging on to Hannah's arm like a limpet while she was walking to my car. Her eyesight at this stage was so bad that being out at night, and particularly a night with such awful weather, was becoming a serious risk for her. I remember noticing the relief in her voice when she said hello and sat into my car, safe and sound. Don't ask me why it took me until then to realise it but realise it I did – I owed her big time. She had sacrificed so much of herself and her own life for me. This was undeniable regardless of what I felt about my disability.

So in that one moment it hit me and I knew that I could no longer put my life at risk – I needed to be as strong as I could be for her. Of course she could live with Dominic, Anne or Liam if anything happened to me but she had said on many occasions that she would be well able to look after herself. I knew now that this was becoming less and less of a reality. I was not in any way being magnanimous; the simple truth was that right now she needed me as I had always needed her. She had never let me down and I was going to do everything in my powers to do the same for her.

So on that miserable December night, I decided that I would, or probably more accurately must, never drink again. I knew cutting down was not an option – it was all or nothing. Just how I was going to find the strength to do this, I had not figured out. I thought of Alcoholics Anonymous. I wasn't sure if I was ready to publicly excoriate myself again, so I decided to try it alone – cold turkey.

Those first few weeks were hard, damned hard, especially with Christmas in between and all that the season of goodwill has come to mean to the Irish drinker's psyche. Shopping in supermarkets, for example, became almost laughable. I would avoid the off-licence section as if it had the plague and the people in it were contagious. Sounds extreme I know and yet, for me at that time, they were. And much as I thought I had developed a hatred of drink, my abstinence from it quickly served to make me re-evaluate my feelings. Alcohol quickly re-invented itself in my head as a long-lost friend whom I had lost touch with and needed to re-acquaint. 'I would love to taste it again, just one more time,' I used to regularly think.

But that is how insidious alcohol and a dependence upon it can be. It can be a great friend to those who treat it with respect. To those of us who don't, it is a sworn enemy.

As the months went on it did get easier. I kept a chart tabulating the days and hours since my last drink, which I updated twice a week, on Sunday and Thursday nights. I still update this chart to this day and will do so forever. It is a great source of encouragement to see the hours and days build up. And those first days, weeks and months were made easier by the fact that not alone did I feel that I was doing this for myself, more importantly I was doing it for Mammy.

Although I have never had it confirmed either medically or sociologically, I have no doubt that I was, am, and always will be, an alcoholic. This is so clearly demonstrated by the incredible unease I feel being around people drinking. It's a feeling of great envy that they are drinking to enjoy themselves whereas all of my drinking was helping me to either cope, just survive, or, incredibly, as a weapon in my aim to die before my mother did. I am always terrified that the temptation to drink again may just prove too strong for me. I fear the thought 'sure I've shown I can stop, just having a drink now and then wouldn't be a problem' but I know it would be.

There is no such thing as an alcoholic cutting down or stopping for periods of time. It is all or nothing. You are merely fooling yourself if you think otherwise. There are no half-measures – a strange choice of words for an alcoholic to use but very apposite.

And incredibly I haven't had any relapses or even near relapses. As I re-read those few words, danger screams out to anyone, me included, with a substance abuse problem. Never take the enemy for granted because when you do it is then that it will rise up and attack.

There aren't many things that I will acknowledge that I am truly proud of in my life, but God am I proud of putting up such a fight against the curse of alcohol dependence, and beating it – for today anyway.

SEVEN

PREPARING TO LET GO

It may sound a little sanctimonious and unreal to say it, but following that fateful day in December 2000 I vowed to give as much of my time as I could to my Ma. I wanted her to live forever. Life without her was just too horrible to contemplate but I was a realist. I knew that nature would eventually intervene. All I could hope was that it would be a long way down the line. I didn't bother praying that when it happened it would be easy – I knew it was going to be anything but.

By and large her health was relatively good for the first couple of years of the new century. She stayed pretty much on familiar territory due to her lack of sight. On my weeks off from work, I would drive her down to morning Mass, which she loved. One thing (amongst many!) which always amazed me about my Ma was that even though she was tested so often during her life, her faith, never, ever wavered. If anything each test put before her seemed to strengthen her faith and belief in God.

At morning Mass, it was so touching and lovely to see the way her friends, knowing that her sight was so compromised, would take care of her in such a discreet, unobtrusive way, particularly at communion time. At the risk of sounding all "touchy-feely," I was always filled with warmth at the goodness and humanity of these people. It also gave me a sense of security. I knew that I should have no fears when she went to Mass alone on my weeks in work.

If she needed to venture any further, such as to a shop for instance, then I would drive her but she would always insist on going into the shop alone. She would not admit to being dependent on me or anyone else in that regard. This is probably just as well as we would have looked a pretty sad sight what with my 'difficulties' and my Ma being virtually blind. Maybe we would have gotten decent discounts! Damn – missed chance!

Weekends were a joy – Saturday would be mapped out. Mammy would prepare the traditional Saturday stew and then we would go to my Da's grave in Palmerstown. When we got back she would go a couple of doors down to our neighbours Tommy and Eileen Byrne for a chat and a cup of tea while I went out and about. I would normally get back around 5 o'clock and we would have the stew together then. I defy anyone on the planet to ever make a stew as delicious as my Ma's stew!

Sunday, as I said earlier, was so special. Dinner together, prepared by both of us, was a time that I would never miss. With the benefit of hindsight, I would give anything, pay anything, to experience it just one more time.

As Liam worked most weekends, he would call in on Sunday for his dinner. I know he used to get some stick from friends that even though he was married, he would still go to his Mammy for dinner! But such was the draw of the woman. No matter where any of us were, she was the focal point of our lives. And as Daryl had spent the first year of his life living in our house, he still spent a lot of weekends staying with his Nanny, after Liam and Mary had moved into their own house. I'm sure that some people may have thought that my eye was wiped while he was around. In fact, it was anything but. I loved seeing my Ma so happy looking after him and spoiling him rotten! If he had been a porcelain doll I don't think that she could have been more protective of him.

With the benefit of hindsight, I can now recall when the real downhill slide started in my Ma's health. It was a couple of weeks before Christmas 2002 when my sense of happiness and contentment were replaced by fear and terror. My Ma would normally get up early on Saturday mornings and would go across the road to have her hair "done". Around 9.30 in the morning of the first Saturday in December, I got a phone call from the hairdresser to say that Mammy had collapsed. I must have been close to breaking the world land speed record in getting to her. It was one of the weekends when Daryl stayed over. I brought him with me and he later said that he had never been in a car going so fast.

When I arrived at the hairdressers she was sitting on a chair. She saw me and greeted me with her usual greeting, "There you are Ger," as if nothing had happened. An ambulance had been called but she refused point-blank to get into it. Instead she said that she would go to see her GP, Dr Forde, whose surgery was only a couple of doors away from the hairdressers. When he examined her, he advised that she should go to hospital as soon as possible to be checked out.

We headed off to the Accident and Emergency Unit in St James's Hospital. Again that journey of barely three miles was filled with fear: fear that this may be the beginning of the end; fear that she may be going on her last ever journey with me. And accompanying these massive, life-changing fears was the fear that I might fall while we were walking into the hospital thus worrying my Ma. I felt so annoyed that my mind should be occupied by a thought like that, at that time, but the fear was there and there was no point then, nor is there now, pretending that it wasn't. I didn't dare speak about anything in the car other than the utterly mundane. There was a lump in my throat and tears in my eyes with the prospect of what lay ahead.

After the standard endless hours of waiting, the hospital diagnosed that she had collapsed due to an adverse reaction to the medication which she'd been on since her heart attack. They changed her medication and discharged her.

While I was relieved that it wasn't something more serious, I had a feeling that it was and that they simply hadn't spotted it. Looking back, I should have listened to my instincts and insisted on more tests. I knew my Ma better than anyone and I just knew that her collapse was not caused by an adverse reaction to medication. The voice of fear that there might be something seriously wrong with her, however, drowned out the screams of my instinct. I developed an ostrich-like approach to it – if I pretended her collapse hadn't happened then maybe it really didn't happen. I was just so utterly scared of losing her.

I'm sure that all four of us knew that something was just not right. I know that I was guilty of having a mentality of 'if I pretend that it isn't there it will go away'. But it wasn't going to. And in fairness to us, my mother was an incredibly independent woman who would listen to advice but would ultimately make her own decision. I think that she was engaging in the "if I pretend it will go away" mentality too and we went along with it.

At the same time she still kept her hospital appointments but perhaps never heeded the clinical advice given there. She attended her GP and the out-patient clinic in St James's regularly. It was discovered that her haemoglobin count was low, due to anaemia, as they thought. Despite being prescribed iron supplements and vitamins, her count continued to drop slowly but steadily. It was obvious that she needed to go into hospital for investigations but she steadfastly refused to and, to my shame and deep, deep regret, I did not encourage or persuade her to do so. She began to lose weight and colour and I remember looking at her on Christmas Day 2003 and thinking, or rather, knowing in my heart that she was not going to be with me for Christmas Day 2004.

Looking back, for all of her hospital out-patient appointments, other family members used accompany my Ma to the hospital. The simple reason for this was that the clinics were always too far for me to walk to. Again, I was also afraid that if I tried to do it and had a mishap getting there then my Ma would get stressed worrying about me. Now looking back, I am so guilty that I didn't get myself a wheelchair and use it to go with her but no, my pride didn't allow me to do that. Could you imagine her allowing pride to prevent her accompanying me if the roles were reversed? Like Hell she would. Jesus, I am so wracked with guilt over that and I know that there is only one person who can assuage that guilt. Hopefully some day she will.

Mammy was prescribed weekly injections aimed at boosting her haemoglobin count. This was tested each week. I prayed like I had never prayed before that each week there would be even the slightest improvement. But there never was. The count continued to go steadily downwards. And yet we both carried on fooling ourselves that eventually things would turn around. I think maybe the damage was already done at that point. Or am I just looking to clear my conscience by saying that?

Following another out-patient appointment in March 2004, Mammy told me that her consultant was adamant that she needed to go into hospital to find out exactly what was causing her low haemoglobin count. She gave me a card and said: "There's his phone number, will you ring him, and he'll explain what they're going to do?"

I made that call on March 10, 2004, a date forever etched on my brain. The doctor's words should not have surprised me yet they rocked me to the core.

"There is something very sinister wrong with your mother and I think you should do everything in your power to persuade her to come into hospital."

I didn't want to ask him the question which I feared most yet I knew that I had to: "Is it cancer?"

Silently I begged: "Please say no. Please. Please say no. Please."

"I would almost certainly say it is," he replied.

I drove home from work that day with such fear. I decided that the "C" word was not going to be used nor was I going to tell anybody else in the family until a definitive confirmation was made.

When I got home, Mammy asked me what the doctor had said. I had told myself so many times on the journey home that under no circumstances was I to become upset, I was to be strong for her, as she had been for me on so many other occasions.

"Did he mention to you that I might have a small growth?" she asked.

So this was going to be the euphemism for "tumour" I thought. I was relieved that she didn't use that word. I couldn't have taken hearing her say it.

"Yes," I said. "I think you should go in and get it sorted once and for all Ma."

The words came out somehow, I don't know how. I felt as if I was secretly planning her death behind her back. I wanted so badly to put my arm around her and say: "Ma, this is bad. I am so scared. Please don't go into hospital. It will go away. In the name of Christ, don't leave me."

She said that she would go in.

I knew she was saying it with great reluctance. She was as scared of leaving me as I was of her leaving me.

There followed weeks of waiting for the hospital to let her know when she was to go in. If I ever suggested that I ring them, or that I arrange for her to be treated privately, she would shout at me angrily in a way that I had never heard her do before. In hindsight, it is obvious that our mutual fears were enormous.

So, wrongly now with the benefit of hindsight, we

waited until she was called into hospital, which she was on May 11, 2004. I knew that I would just not be able to bring her to hospital that day. For once it was not because of any restrictions caused by my disability, it was simply that I could not bear to be the person to bring her from the house on what I was now convinced was a journey that she would never return from. So Anne brought her and I wished her well from the front door.

Even though I had told her that I would be in to the hospital in a couple of hours, Mammy hugged me before she left like she had never hugged me before. I tried, like I have never tried before, to keep a stiff upper lip while she was getting ready to go and when she was leaving. I think I managed it.

When they had gone, and the car was out of view, I went back inside to the sitting room, to the table where we had shared so many breakfasts, dinners and teas together. I slumped to the ground and sobbed uncontrollably.

I gave Mammy a few hours to get settled into the hospital before I went to see her that afternoon. I was so shocked when I saw her. Incredibly, in those few short hours, she seemed to have deteriorated so much and looked so desperately ill now.

The doctors explained that she would have to undergo an endoscopy and colonoscopy to find out exactly what was happening. To ensure that the tests would show up clear results, it was necessary for my Ma's bowels to be completely empty. This would be done by way of her drinking several litres of a substance, which she described as "foul".

To watch your mother, frail through illness, lost through lack of sight, go through this torture was heartbreaking.

She went through this on the Thursday after she was admitted to hospital in preparation for the tests to be done the following day. I swear to God, if I could, I would have gone through it a hundred times over for her.

Cruelly, unforgivably cruelly, due to an administrative error, her name wasn't put down on the list for scoping that day. This meant that she was re-scheduled for the next week, resulting in her having to go through this horror all over again. Such mismanagement of a simple administrative process is an indictment of the management of health care in this country. Try as I may, I find no mitigating circumstances to justify such appalling public service. Although at times I am far too timid and easily intimidated by authority, I was so incensed by this that I absolutely hit the roof.

I asked to speak to the doctor who had made the error and for some convenient reason he said that he couldn't come to the ward to see me, nor could he speak to me on the phone. It is probably just as well. I wouldn't have been responsible for what I would have done to the person who had put my mother through this. So the poor nursing staff had to listen, as I let rip. And yet all they could do was apologise and say that the same thing would not happen again when the tests were re-scheduled.

That Friday there was an awful lot of activity on the ward as I was giving vent to the staff about the cancellation. When I had calmed down, I asked what was going on. I was told that this was a "five-day" ward and that it was closing down for the weekend. My mother was to be moved to another ward – to Hospital Five on the other side of the St James's Campus. Ambulance officers were moving hither and thither helping patients who were too ill to move by themselves, one of which was my Ma. I quickly realised I wouldn't be able to keep up with them so I told Mammy that I would follow them over to Hospital Five.

I walked as fast as I could and found Mammy sitting in a wheelchair by herself, on one of the long, ridiculously long, corridors in St James's. When I spoke to her she got a bit of a fright and I had to reassure her that it was me. She said that the ambulance man had said he would be back for her. Unusually for her, such a strong, independent woman, she said to me in a barely audible, broken voice: "Don't leave me Ger."

We got to Hospital Five eventually – a more opposite scene to the modern ward we had left was unimaginable. I could not believe the squalor and there was no other word to describe it. The smell of shit, piss and dirt, hit you when you walked onto the ward. There wasn't even a chair beside my Ma's bed for her to sit in. I had to use some Department of Health influence to get her one on the Monday.

As my Ma tried to settle in I was flabbergasted. I spent the rest of the weekend ringing private hospitals to see if she could be transferred. Alas, the Irish disease of Healthcare effectively closing down for the weekend kicked in and she had to stay there. I later complained to hospital management that you wouldn't kennel dogs in such conditions. They took the standard line of lack of resources and prioritisation of such resources. But given the fact that it was my mother who was being affected by this, it cut no ice with me. At the time, though, I didn't know what to do. I wanted to bring Mammy home yet I knew in my heart that she was just too ill for that to happen.

When the other three arrived, they were as shocked as I was that we were going to have to leave our mother in that ward. The feeling of complete helplessness was shared by us all.

As sick and weak as she was, her instinct to worry about me did not leave her. For the next morning the phone rang at about 8.30 am.

A nurse from the hospital said: "Gerard this is nurse so and so from St James's. There's absolutely nothing to worry about. Your mother is here beside me. She just wants to have a chat with you."

She then handed the phone to my Ma.

"There ya are Ger," Mammy said. "Are you alright?"

"Yeah I'm grand," I said. "Are you?"

"I'm fine," she said. "I don't want you to be worrying about me, do you hear me?"

We spoke for anotehr few minutes. Just hearing her voice, cheered me at a time when I had barely slept through worry. It was as if by some sort of symbiosis she knew how I was feeling and was anxious to reassure me. And not for the first time, she did.

Incredibly, however, she settled in and seemed to be happier there than in the first ward, so I decided that once she was content, then I should be also.

There were two other women on the ward with her. One of them was always in bed – what her condition was I never knew. She never seemed to have any visitors calling in to see her. One day she asked me if I could bring her a newspaper some time as she loved to read. After that I used to bring her a few newspapers and magazines everyday. As her bed was close to the door she was able to see visitors coming. Everyday when she'd see me she'd say in her loud voice: "Here's Gerard, Nellie."

God, I'm such a hit with the ladies!

One evening she scared me when she called me over to her and said that my Ma had asked her earlier that day who was standing at the door of the ward. When she told my Ma that there wasn't anybody there, Mammy had said: "I thought it was Willie."

"Who's Willie?" the lady asked.

"My husband," Mammy replied.

My mind immediately raced back to the last days of my father's life when he had said that his late mother had visited him in hospital. I had viewed this later as a mother coming to reclaim her son. Was my father now coming to take my Ma back, after nearly 18 years of separation through death? I silently pleaded with him: "Not yet, not yet."

The other woman on the ward used to drive Mammy demented! She would wander around all day and night. Where she got the energy from, I'll never know. I never saw her sitting still for more than a couple of minutes!

The tests did take place a few days later, but they, and the preparation for them, took so much out of Mammy. The results were not good and my worst fears were realised. A tumour was discovered. I was told that they simply had to operate to try to remove it as if they left it as it was, chances were that Mammy would "die screaming in agony".

In consultation with her doctor we decided to tell her that they had found a growth which needed to be operated on. As a family, we sat with her while the doctor

explained it to her. If I live to be 100, I will never forget
the low, submissive, totally trusting tone in her voice as she
asked him questions. I felt an overwhelming urge to put
my arms around her and tell the world to go away that I
would look after her. Yet I knew that if she was to regain
any semblance of a quality of life, then surgery really was
the only option.

The following Thursday, the surgeons attempted to
remove the tumour. For some reason, which I still can't
understand, I decided to go to work rather than be at the
hospital. Anne stayed with Mammy that morning while
they prepared her for surgery. She said that seeing Mammy
being wheeled down to the operating theatre broke her
heart. She went home to her kids as the doctors said the
surgery would last for many hours. Unable to concentrate,
I decided to leave work early and head to the hospital. For
the first and only time in over 20 years that I had worked
in Hawkins House, the electricity had been cut off as a
result of a major power failure in Dublin City Centre.
Given the fact that I worked on the 11th floor, 22 flights
of stairs up, I had no option but to wait patiently for the
power to return. When it did, I drove at breakneck pace
to St James's.

Just as I arrived onto the corridor of Ma's ward, she
was being wheeled back from the operating theatre to the
High Dependency Unit (HDU). I barely recognised her. I
remember saying aloud: "Jesus she's dead."

I waited outside the HDU while the medics settled
her. Her consultant came out and said words which
reverberated around my head: "It's not looking good. The
tumour was too extensive so we couldn't remove it."

I asked him was she going to die, begging in my head

for him to say: "Don't be silly, of course she's not."

But he didn't.

"Yes," he replied.

"When?" I asked.

He said that there was no guarantee that she would make it through the night ahead. "She is 81 you know," he added in a matter-of-fact way, as if he were talking about a vintage car.

I replied in an angry and very broken voice: "She's also my mother."

I walked away. I just needed to see her. As the High Dependency Unit treats critically ill patients, you are required to almost don a space suit before entering. So I gowned up and went inside the HDU.

Mammy was wrapped in tinfoil, an oxygen mask on her face. A few days after she had been admitted to hospital, I had collected a new calliper. I had completely forgotten that I had told her about it. When she saw me in the HDU, her first words, in such a hoarse voice from tubes which had just been removed from her throat, were: "There ye are Ger, and you got a new calliper?"

Uncharacteristically for me, I somehow didn't cry, I kept it together and said: "Yeah, it's great."

Even at this moment of great peril, when her life was literally in great danger, her first thoughts were not for herself but for me. My heart was breaking and it was all I could do to prevent a flood of tears from coming.

But it was Mammy who sobbed then and I begged her not to cry. I told her that she would be fine. She held my hand in a vice-like grip. I knew the longer I stayed, the more likely I was to break down, which would have been so wrong, as it would have affected Mammy deeply.

I said that I would let her sleep and that I would be back later. I knew she didn't want me to go yet I knew for both our sakes that I should.

I kissed her goodbye and walked towards the door, telling myself just to go and not look back. But I did look back and somehow she raised her hand to wave goodbye to me.

Once out of view, I was consumed by the utter bleakness and horror of what was happening. I literally had to be helped by the nurses to a waiting chair in the corridor. Alone, with the work of the ward going on, with visitors coming and going, with evening tea being delivered to patients, I sat by myself, lonelier than I had ever felt in my life, and cried like I've never cried before.

The others arrived, I'm sure, very soon afterwards. Time meant nothing to me. I was in a haze of total and complete sadness. Seeing each of them going, in turn, to see Mammy made me worse. I had prepared them as best I could for how ill she looked, but no amount of preparation could help them. My head was all over the place. I wanted to get as far away from the hospital as possible while also wanting to stay with Mammy.

No matter what anyone said or did I was completely inconsolable. I didn't care who saw me in this almost hysterical state. All I knew, all I cared about was that the light of my life, my true, and yes my only, reason for living, was slipping slowly away.

EIGHT

I'LL BE ALRIGHT MA

Against the predictions of the doctors on that horrible Thursday, Mammy did last through the night. In fact she rallied so well that she was moved from the High Dependency Unit back onto the main ward within a couple of days. When I saw her back on the ward I remember thinking that she looked better than I had seen her look for such a long time. And yet the memory of her consultant's opinion kept coming back to me. I just couldn't square the circle of his doom-laden view with just how well Mammy looked.

"They could be wrong," I kept telling myself. "They don't know my Ma."

Mammy was kept in hospital for a couple more weeks. When somebody is in hospital for that length of time, you get to know the other patients on the ward and their families. I always got the impression that they just knew or sensed how ill Mammy was by their extremely well-meaning questions and looks. I don't mean that in any negative sense. I think they saw Mammy and how concerned we were and may have thought 'there but for the Grace of God go I'.

On the weeks when I was in work, I always tried to get to the hospital as the early evening meal arrived. Mammy's sight difficulties seemed to be accentuated in this strange environment. And so, I knew, that without anyone being there to feed her she wouldn't eat and, therefore, wouldn't regain any semblance of strength. And again, the very act of having to feed her was heart-breaking. Here was this incredibly independent woman depending upon such basic help. While I was filled with pride and gratitude to be able to help her in this way, I was also filled with frustration at the unfairness of it all.

Any conversations I had with doctors about her progress always seemed to include the words "Hospice Care" in them. I asked so many times about chemotherapy and radiotherapy and I just knew by the way they completely dismissed my queries, as if I was being almost fanciful, that she was beyond hope of such intervention. I told them under no circumstances was anyone ever to use the word "Hospice" when talking to her. This wasn't because I was trying to pretend that all of this wasn't really happening, or that I was being patronising to her in any way. I just wanted to protect her in every possible way, to give her hope, false hope yes, but hope that I myself did not now have.

In those couple of weeks after the operation, Mammy seemed to be regaining her old self and it was obvious that she was really trying to do so. As her strength grew, she would walk up and down the long ward corridor, linking someone's arm at all times. I used to feel so incredibly jealous of the people who could walk her up and down the corridor. I knew for me to do so would have been too risky, as one stumble or slip from me would have seriously endangered her.

I raged to myself: "Damn this fucking disability. It's even now denying me a precious memory, one I could keep forever, of such closeness with my Ma – of my physically protecting her." What I wouldn't have given just to be able-bodied for half an hour. I would have loved to have felt her arm in mine – me protecting her now.

I know she would have loved it, and it would have helped me enormously in coping with what was happening. However, not for the first or for the last time, I was a spectator, frustrated by this gift, given to me by God.

I wanted so badly to believe that the doctors were wrong about Mammy. I badgered them at every opportunity, asking them to revise their opinions, questioning again whether chemotherapy or radiotherapy would help, only to be told there was no point. They were clear that it was now a matter of quality, rather than length, of life.

Finally, two weeks after the operation, again on a Thursday (why does every crisis in my life seem to happen on Thursdays?), Mammy was discharged from hospital. Anne and myself went in to collect her.

I was filled with trepidation, wondering if we could give her the care that she was going to need. The four of us had discussed this when Mammy's discharge from hospital was first suggested. We'd agreed that together we would do everything in our powers to look after her at home. Before we left, Anne and I were met by a member of the hospital's Palliative Care Team. Any last bit of hope or optimism was quickly taken away from me by her first question: "Do you want your mother to die at home?"

It was a very functional, practical question. The significance of its asking, and its answer, scared me beyond belief.

Without needing to think about it, Anne and me both said yes and were assured that every resource would be in place to allow this to happen. The Hospice (Jesus that word – "Stop saying it," I begged this young girl in my mind) would contact us and make the necessary arrangements. When she was finished outlining Mammy's care plan, the Team Worker asked me if I was alright.

I said yes when really I had never felt less alright in my life.

I asked her and Anne if I could have a few minutes by myself. I felt as if I was about to be convulsed in tears. And yet when they left I didn't cry – I sat there alone, wondering was I going to be able to cope with what were sure to be traumatic weeks ahead. I told myself I had to because there was somebody who was a damned sight more important than me in all this – my Ma.

We drove home. I sensed that my Ma may well have begun to wonder why she was being discharged from hospital when she was still obviously far from well. Thankfully she didn't question me on this, as I would not have been able to answer her without breaking down.

The thought that this was more than likely the last time that I would be driving Mammy anywhere really choked me. This was the second time I had experienced that thought when about to lose a parent. With my Da I felt just unnaturally awful, but with my Ma, given all we'd been through, I felt so much worse. It was a relatively quiet journey, with Anne trying her best to lighten the mood.

When we reached home, Dominic and Liam were there. They helped Mammy in and for the first time, I saw a look in her eyes that told me that time was at a very serious premium. You know when someone you love is close to death without any medic confirming it for you – you feel it in your heart. Your heart beats faster and then seems to stop, then fast and so on. I got that feeling then.

Mammy settled back home. A normally busy woman around the house, instead she was now only able to sit in her chair by the sitting room table, where she loved to be. She'd always really enjoyed grandchildren staying overnight, with the result that there was a single bed in her room, ready at all times for them. I asked her if she would like me to sleep there, half-expecting her to say: "Would you get away outa that."

Instead she said: "I'd love that."

And so I did. Some nights I stayed awake all night in case she roused needing anything. Some nights we would talk and laugh about things for ages, with the street lights outside the only light in the room. I cherished those times then and I treasure the memories of them now.

The Hospice Home Care Team visited. Dr Cunningham from the Hospice was the first to arrive. After she spoke to Mammy, she came downstairs and spoke to me alone. She asked me how I was coping and I said as best I could. I said that I just couldn't get used to the fact that my mother would soon not be with me anymore. I deliberately said the next few words hoping that Dr Cunningham would give me hope – "I'd love to think that my mother will still be here in six months."

To which she replied: "Six months is a long way off for your mother."

I knew then just how short the time frame undoubtedly was. I knew that if there was one thing you can be guaranteed it is that a Hospice doctor knows about dying and death. The doctor's words were stark, carefully chosen and ultimately correct. She knew, I'm sure, why I asked her the question. I was looking for hope where none existed. And it would have been wrong of her to pretend otherwise. But her words sank my heart further, if that were possible.

Before the doctor arrived, I had to invent a story for Mammy. I told her that the medical team calling in was a normal follow up by the hospital for people who have had a major operation. She accepted what I said. Or did she know and was just hoping that this was what I thought? As ever, she was protecting me while I was protecting her.

Dr Cunningham prescribed steroids for Mammy, saying that these would help her. And boy did they. They seemed to give her an insatiable appetite and incredible physical strength. Whereas when she first came home from hospital she struggled up and down the stairs, now she did that journey in jig time. False optimism again sneaked back into my head.

I spent as much time with her as was humanly possible, interrupted only by intermittent days in work. Then one lunch time I was at the cooker making some soup for the two of us, when she said: "Ger, I need to talk to you."

"About what?" I asked casually, totally unprepared for what her answer turned out to be.

"My funeral," she said.

I had my back to her and it was as if someone had switched my tear ducts on to full blast. I admonished myself in my head, saying: "If you cry now in front of her you will just be proving what kind of a selfish bastard you are."

So I got myself together, turned around and said: "Okay, if that's what you want, we'll talk now."

I can't begin to describe how heartbreakingly difficult the conversation was. And yet if someone had walked in on it they could be forgiven for assuming that the conversation was as trivial as two people sorting out their weekly shopping list – Mammy dictating, me with pen and paper at the ready. She was so clear in her directions. She knew who she wanted to carry her coffin, making sure to include her two eldest grandchildren, Ciarán and Daryl; two of her other grandsons Liam and Fionn should be carrying candles as her coffin was being brought into and from the church; and those candles should then be given to her brother, Dave, at the end of the funeral mass. God how she loved Dave – if my sister loves me half as much as my Ma loved Dave then I am one lucky person.

She wanted Dave's son, Paul, to do a reading, with Lorraine, a friend of ours, to do the second reading. She wanted the remaining grandchildren, Jennifer, Adam, Ellen and Cathal, to do Prayers of the Faithful or to bring up the Offertory Gifts.

I asked if she wanted to be brought to a funeral parlour the night before, to which she said: "No, I'd love to stay here if you don't mind."

If I didn't mind.

I somehow managed to ask her if she wanted any

particular music played at her funeral mass.

She said that she would leave that up to me but that she would like to have *Ave Maria* sung.

"But it has to be Gunot's version!" she said.

In a strange way, I was so happy that we had had that chat. I knew then that she was aware that her time was short. It was now my duty, in that short time, to show her, to tell her and to convince her, that I would be okay. I needed her to know that all the work that she had put in would stand me in good stead. I am not going to say that I stoically carried out my duties. Hardly an hour passed without me weeping privately because of what was happening and what was about to happen.

Anne's three children and Liam's five visited her regularly over the final weeks. I'm not sure if they took in exactly what was happening, especially the younger ones. One particular day, Daryl and young Liam called to see her. They sat and chatted with her for a while but she tired easily then. After she dozed off they came downstairs – their young faces were etched with confusion and sadness.

Daryl unexpectedly, asked me: "How long has Nanny got to live?"

How do you answer a question like that? Do you soft-soap the answer? I decided not to bullshit them.

"I don't know for sure Daryl," I said, "but we're not going to have her here for Christmas."

They looked shocked, appalled and utterly sad. The three of us sat there without saying much. Each one, I'm sure, fearing that one of us would start crying which would start us all off.

At that time, Liam's sister-in-law, Áine, was making

the same sad, painful journey from this life as Mammy. A beautiful girl of just 40 years of age, she was similarly cursed with cancer. Cancer is a merciless taker of young and old alike. So Daryl and Liam were witnessing their auntie and their grandmother both slipping slowly away. It's small wonder then that they were confused.

I was about to tell them about the conversation I had had with my Ma about her funeral and the role that she wanted them to take in it. But one look at young Liam's face told me not to. He had a look of anger, mixed with incredible sadness and who could blame him. I decided to leave it.

A few days after Mammy came home from hospital, an appointment card arrived from St James's. It advised that she had an out-patient appointment with her consultant the following week. It seemed such a normal event in what was anything but a normal time. Myself and Dominic went with her to the hospital – Dominic brought her to the clinic as the curse of the long walk overtook me. When the consultant saw Mammy he turned to one of his team and said: "I thought we referred this woman to the Hospice."

Dominic wasn't sure if Mammy heard – I hope and pray she didn't. When Dominic pointed out that the hospital had sent out the appointment card to attend at his clinic, the consultant said that all he could do was admit her and administer a blood transfusion which "might give her a little more time".

Naturally Dominic accepted.

And so Mammy was admitted. I stayed with her for much of the day. Two junior doctors attempted to take blood samples from her but as she was in such decline, they found it very difficult to find a vein in her arm. The result was that by the time they eventually succeeded, her arm was horribly bruised. I had to leave the room for a few minutes when I saw this as I was boiling with anger – anger at them for making such a mess and anger at God, wherever the Hell He was or, in fact, if there actually was a God, overseeing this misery.

It broke my heart leaving Mammy that evening. In truth, I shouldn't have left her. There was no reason to go as Mammy had been admitted to a private room while the blood was being transfused, so I could have slept in a chair. But I just knew that had I stayed, Mammy would have been more concerned about me than herself, so very reluctantly I headed home.

We collected her the next day. I'll never forget the look on her face when Dominic brought her out of the hospital. When she saw me she smiled so wide and when she reached me she threw her arms around me. It was as if she hadn't seen me for months, instead of just a few hours. Despite the transfusion, her condition did not show any significant improvement. In fact, when we got her home the whole effort had tired her so much that she asked to go straight to bed and was asleep within seconds.

I sat by her bed while she slept and silently promised her that I would not let her go through that again. Further transfusions might perhaps prolong her life but I would be doing that for me and not for her. I knew that that would be so wrong.

I kept thinking about the words that the Palliative Care Team worker had said to myself and Anne the day Mammy was being discharged from St James's: "There will be some lovely memories to share with your Mam over

And what exactly is wrong with a boy playing with a doll's house!

My home from home as a child – St Joseph's Ward, Our Lady's Hospital, Crumlin, Dublin.

(Reproduced courtesy of Our Lady's Children's Hospital, Crumlin)

Mammy (before her change in hair colour!) as ever with a protective arm around me.

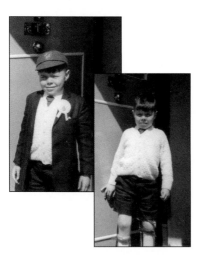

First Communion Day – wouldn't you run away with him! How brave was I wearing short trousers?

Myself and Ben, around 1990. We're in the Phoenix Park and I'm holding on to him for dear life as he surveys potential prey!

Dominican Convent, Ballyfermot, in the early 1970s. Mammy with her co-worker Alma, the nuns and the parish curate, Father Michael Cleary.

Above: Liam Jnr, Cathal, Adam, Jenny and Daryl.

Left: Fionn, Ellen and Ciarán.

This is my favourite photograph of my Ma and Da – they just look so happy.

the next few weeks so make sure that you enjoy them."

In my heart of hearts I knew that she was merely voicing aloud something she had read or studied. I'm sure that she was trying to give us some consolation, where, in truth, none existed. I knew that there were going to be no lovely memories, how could there be? What lovely memory can you have of watching the most important person in your life slip slowly but surely from you? How can you possibly have any good memories from a time when you are battling against a virulent disease which is intent on taking the life of the person you love most in the world?

About a week after the blood transfusion, one morning Mammy said that she had had a dream the previous night that the two of us had gone for a drive to the Phoenix Park. In desperation, I saw that this might be the chance to perhaps get a "lovely memory" in the midst of the nightmare that was unfolding. As it was a beautiful, sunny day I suggested that maybe we should go for a drive down to the Park that afternoon. I was so pleasantly surprised when Mammy agreed.

As the day wore on, however, her enthusiasm for the short journey waned. Instead of leaving it, I pushed and pushed until she agreed to go, even though I knew that she was neither in mental or physical form for it. I was just so desperate to have something good to look back on when I remembered these awful weeks.

Even walking the 20 or so steps to my car and then getting into it was such a struggle for her. We drove to the Park, with me pathetically trying to reminisce with her about days gone by and her feeling so uncomfortable and in pain. I'm sure she just wanted to be back home in her bed.

We stayed out for less than half an hour and Mammy was so relieved when I suggested that we go home. Her struggle to get out of the car and back into the house was ten times harder than the outward journey. I was burning with anger when I put her safely back to bed; anger at God for denying me just one last happy time with Mammy and so angry with myself for being so selfish, all because I was trying to achieve that happy memory. If only I could turn back time so that I could undo that day. God love her, I'm sure she knew what I was trying to do and she in turn was trying as best as she possibly could to give me that last piece of happiness. But her body, now shutting down at such an alarming rate, would not allow her to do it for me.

* * * *

As the weeks passed we devised an informal rota system so that we could take turns caring for Mammy. This was important even though it wasn't that physically tiring, as, God love her, she was as undemanding in ill-health as she had been in good health. It was the mental tiredness which was so hard to cope with. The energy sapping knowledge of her illness and what direction it was taking her was terrible – unspeakably terrible.

And with the benefit of hindsight the mistake we made was not talking to each other about how we were feeling – and I was as guilty of this as anyone. Whether it would have helped? We'll never know. But we were all consumed by our own thoughts and fears, mainly fears, of what was unfolding before our eyes and how helpless we were at its unfolding.

Sadly, from early August on, Mammy became very confused. The resonances that this had with the last days of my father's life were so vivid. Normal conversation became difficult and, at times, impossible.

I always used to get a great buzz every week from giving my Ma her share of my wages from work. I don't think she ever once took it without a fight but I got such a kick out of knowing that I was "the bread-winner" in the house. As soon as Mammy came home from hospital, I resumed this. Yet in that first week in August when I gave her my money she gave it back to me saying: "You hold on to it Ger. I don't know what to do with it anymore."

How something which may sound so trivial could rip through my world as it did, I'll never forget. And yet it was just another of the signs that she was leaving. In truth, it really was as if she had already died, yet her body was still visible to us.

Despite incredible physical and mental fatigue, we cared for her to the best of our abilities. I tried to spend every moment I could with her, knowing how precious those moments were. I had always maintained that she should remain at home for as long as her comfort was not compromised in any way. And yet even trying to spend as much time as possible with Mammy was heartbreaking. It was because although the person I was spending so much time with was my beloved Mother, in so many ways it wasn't her. She was now so ravaged by this cursed illness that my time with her was being consumed by my feelings of horror – horror that she was going through this and that there was not a thing that I could do about it. This was clearly shown when I asked one of the Hospice nurses how long she thought Mammy would have to endure this.

"It could go on for weeks," she said.

Dominic said that the look of horror on my face when she said this was incredible.

And I was horrified that Mammy would have to endure this for much longer. And I also felt such guilt. I was guilty of wanting this torment to end for her. Even though I knew that the only way it was going to end was for Mammy to die. And I was also guilty that even though she was so sick, I just wanted her to stay with me at all costs. 'How could I be so cruel?' I thought, 'knowing that she would be in pain and discomfort, just so that I didn't have to lose her. Was I being selfish? Was this a sign of just how much I loved her and was going to miss her? Maybe the answer to both questions is yes. All I know is that my head was all over the place. I was like Jesus in the Garden of Gethsemane – I wanted this torment to pass. I wanted my mother to be well again. I just wanted this Hell to be over.

Sunday, August 22, the 18th anniversary of my father's death arrived. Mammy was so restless that day. She neither wanted to be up or in bed. The feeling of helplessness and hopelessness I felt that day is difficult to describe. My despair at what was happening and my inability to stop it conspired to make this one of the worst days of my life. While I had friends and family to talk to, right at that time I would have loved to have had that 'special someone' to hold me, to tell me everything was going to be alright – to just be with me at these darkest hours of my life.

That night, I went up to see if Mammy needed anything and found her sitting at the side of her bed. I asked her if she was alright and suddenly she started sobbing. All of the confusion in her mind over the previous days seemed to disappear, as she poured out her heart to me, like never before.

"I'm so ashamed of myself Ger," she said. "I can't even make it to the toilet without someone helping me."

I sat down beside her and put my arms around her. She had lost so much weight that her now tiny frame was lost in my embrace.

"You have nothing, nothing to be ashamed of," I told her. "You know that you would be the first person to help us if we needed it."

I tried to think of words which might console her as she sobbed but I couldn't find any, for there were none to find. Instead I just sobbed with her. We sat there for ages, just crying and crying – me for her, her for me, I'm sure.

The next day I got up for work. Mammy was in a deep sleep. Before leaving I went up to see her, to say goodbye for the day. She was awake and for the first time ever she asked me if I really had to go to work.

I said that I did as I had been taking a lot of time off recently. She asked if I could come home early and I promised that I would.

I did come home early. Dominic was looking after Mammy and when I came into the house, his face was ashen. He said it had been an awful day. Mammy had a massive haemorrhage in the toilet earlier. We were never sure whether her bowel had burst or what exactly had gone wrong but whatever happened shook Dominic badly. I felt so guilty for having gone to work.

Mammy was in bed when I went up to her. She seemed to either have no recollection of what had happened earlier or was trying to pretend that it hadn't happened, possibly fearing that it might mean returning to hospital.

I rang Dr Forde and asked him to come see her.

He arrived shortly afterwards and when he'd examined her he suggested that maybe she should be brought to Accident & Emergency.

"What would they do for her?" I asked him

He explained that they would re-hydrate her but that that would be all they could do. When he confirmed that she wasn't in pain, there was no way that I was letting her go to the hospital. The thought of her dying on a trolley in a corridor or in a crowded A & E, was just not going to happen. I was determined that she was going to die with dignity in her own bed.

As I wasn't sure what direction this was going now or at what speed, I rang Anne and Liam and advised that they get to the house as soon as possible. When they did, the four of us agreed that Mammy should stay at home.

I told Dr Forde what Mammy had said about me going to work that morning. He said that I should stay close to my Ma as much as possible from now on. The meaning behind his unspoken words was crushing.

All that night I tossed and turned. I had begun to wonder if my desire for her to be at home was not jeopardising her comfort now. So, the following day I spoke to the Hospice about this.

I'll never forget the conversation myself and Dominic had with Karen from the Hospice in our sitting room, while Mammy slept upstairs. Karen agreed that having spoken to the nurses from the Home Care Team they all felt that my Ma should be brought in to the Hospice. I felt like such a traitor, talking about Mammy behind her back. It felt as if we were almost conspiring for her to be looked after by someone else. Karen, in such a compassionate, yet thoroughly professional way, made me see that I was being selfless rather than selfish.

I said that I wouldn't be able to face seeing Mammy leaving the house to go to the Hospice, knowing that this time, without any shadow of doubt, she would never be coming back.

Karen suggested that maybe I could go to the Hospice and be there when Mammy arrived. I thought about this and agreed that this was the best solution to an utterly hopeless situation. Dominic agreed.

However, even in the hour or so that we were talking, Mammy's condition had worsened considerably. It became quickly obvious that moving her to the Hospice had, in that short space of time, become unrealistic.

Over the next few days Mammy slept more often. The Hospice Team decided that steroids should be withdrawn and a morphine pump inserted. From Tuesday, August 24, Mammy's speech gradually went.

That evening, Anne and Liam helped her into the toilet. I stood by the window as they held her so tenderly on the way back to her bed. I smiled at her, yet she showed absolutely no reaction. It would be wrong to say that she looked through me as I knew in that instant that her sight was now completely gone. It was the last time that my mother left her bed.

I kept asking her if she was happy and she nodded her head yes. I knew that I was asking more for me than for her.

During that week, while the four of us were around her bed, she looked at me and asked in a barely audible voice: "What's happening to me?"

I was terrified in that instant. Without thinking, and from my heart, I asked her if she really wanted to know.

"Yes," she said emphatically and as clearly as she possibly could.

So without preparation and as unemotionally as I could I asked her: "You believe in God don't you? And you believe in Our Lady?"

She nodded twice.

"And you believe that Daddy is in Heaven with Them waiting for you?"

Again she nodded.

"Well you're going to be with them very soon."

I don't know where I got the strength to say it, and to this day I don't know whether I was right either to say it or in the way I said it, but there was no going back now. I'm not even sure if the other three agreed with me being so forthright, especially Anne who looked aghast. She stared at me as if I was re-enacting a horrible deathbed scene from an old black and white movie. But the look in Mammy's face when she'd asked me what was happening was one of sheer fear. I could not, would not, let her be fearful at this time. I knew her faith was always so important to her. I wanted her to know that that faith was about to be rewarded. There is only one person who can say if my answer was right and that is Mammy. That said I still struggle with the decision I made and will continue to do so until I see her again because I know it broke my heart saying it to her.

Conversations with Mammy after this were very limited – you spoke but she was now unable to do so. The last conversation I had with her is etched on my heart and in my head. I was alone in the room with her, sitting by her bed. She was wide awake. I asked her if she was happy – again probably seeking reassurance for myself.

When she nodded yes, I asked her if she was worried about anything. She turned her head towards me and I expected her to nod again. However, she smiled slightly but it was not a happy smile. It was more a concerned smile if that doesn't sound paradoxical.

"What is it?" I asked. "Is it me?"

She nodded yes, half-smiling, half-crying.

I took her hand and said: "Please Ma, don't worry about me – I'll be alright. I promise you that with all my heart."

I asked her if she believed me and again she nodded.

I hope she did because I know that I didn't believe me. I knew that I was not going to be alright. Of course, the functional day-to-day things would not be a problem. But who was I going to turn to in times of crisis, for nobody, nobody understood me the way she did. But right at that particular time, I was damned if I was going to cause her any more worry than I had over the previous 40 odd years.

Shortly after she was discharged from hospital, the District Nurse had called to see her. While she was talking to Mammy, I noticed a form at the top of my mother's file which had obviously been completed just prior to her discharge from hospital. One of the questions on the form read: 'What fears does the patient have regarding his/her illness.'

To which my mother had replied: 'How my youngest son would cope if I died.'

My emotions were mixed on reading this. I was annoyed that I hadn't yet proven to her how independent

I could be and I was frustrated with her that she was worrying about me at a time when she should have been devoting that time to herself. But my overriding emotion was one of incredible love. It was so like her to be worrying about me at a time when, for once, she should have been worrying about herself. But when did she ever put herself before me?

The day after it was decided that Mammy was just too weak to be moved to the Hospice, the Home Care Team decided that we needed a Night Nurse to look after her. This would allow us to get some sleep as well as we were all completely exhausted. I remember the first night that the nurse came very clearly. I was highly indignant when she ushered me from Mammy's room, telling me to go and get some sleep. I was sure that I would be awake all night worrying about Mammy but once my head hit the pillow, I fell asleep immediately. Yet, remembering how it had been with my father, over 18 years before, I knew that once night nurses were installed time was quickly running out.

The next few days and nights were horrific, simply horrific. Mammy spent much of the time sleeping, in mini-comas almost. Her breathing was so laboured and incredibly distressing to listen to. Each time you left her room you wondered if she would be alive the next time you saw her. The Home Care Team increased the morphine in the pump to ensure that she would not be in any pain but doing this also deepened her sleep.

I was sitting by her bed during one of those days, just holding her hand telling her I was there, when the thought struck me that I would never again sit down and have a chat with her. I used to enjoy nothing better than coming home from work in the evening, when she would fill me in on all the local gossip she may have heard that day, or I would bend her ear about something which had cheesed me off in work. And I loved mealtimes that we shared together, or reading out articles in the newspaper which I thought might interest her. Simple, utterly simple pleasures, which in that moment I realised that I would never, ever have again.

I was so angry with God, that he was putting Mammy, one of his most loyal and faithful servants, through this torture. I don't know whether my anger had increased or dissipated when during this week, I said to the others that I thought we should get a priest to give Mammy the Last Rites. Even saying it aloud, at that time, tore me to pieces. It was such a demonstrative act. I was acknowledging that I was losing her and I just knew that it was what she would have wanted me to do for her. They agreed and one of the priests from the parish, Father Roy, called to the house. As he stood beside Mammy's bed, he began in a low voice: "In the name of the Father, and of the Son, and of the Holy Spirit."

And hearing those words, in her unconscious, virtual comatose state, Mammy slowly raised her right hand to her forehead to bless herself. She was so ill and weak that she was unable to complete the blessing but her devotion and faith shone through in this simple gesture.

I couldn't stay in the room. Just seeing her trying to bless herself had come so unexpectedly that it broke me in two. But in a weird way I was happy that she wasn't angry with God in the same way that I was. She was accepting of His will in a way that I could never be.

Those last days were also just a few days away from

my birthday. For some reason, I hoped that she would last until then and pass away on that day. It was as if it would have been further proof of the special bond that we shared. It was an irrational thought I know. In any event, did I really need any further proof of that bond which I knew that death was about to break? I said this to one of the Home Care nurses and she said that she didn't think that Mammy would be able to last that long.

Saturday, August 28, came. Mammy's breathing was unbearably distressing to hear. The nurses kept telling us that it wasn't as upsetting for Mammy, and I pray to God they were right. The night nurse came and felt that time was moving on and it was coming near the end. She said that she would call us if there was any change in Mammy's condition during the night.

At around 4.30 am I heard my bedroom door opening – before Dominic could call out my name I had jumped up out of bed. I pleaded with God: "Not now – please not yet."

I could hear Mammy's breathing as I approached her bedroom door. It was so very different to how it had sounded just a few short hours previously. She seemed to be breathing in very heavily without appearing to be breathing out. It was awful – just too horrible for words. I begged God for this not to be my last memories of her.

At around 6 am, Pearl, the night nurse, said that Mammy had settled a little and that the crisis had passed.

We all left the room. I don't think any of us felt like sleep now. We were each lost in our own thoughts. I knew that the moment that I had dreaded happening all of my life, was not too far away.

Sunday, August 29, dawned bright and breezy outside – but inside the unwelcome visitor of God was coming to reclaim one of his own. Mammy's GP, Dr Forde, called in at around noon while the Hospice nurse was with her. They were with her for a while as the four of us waited downstairs.

The nurse left, saying that we should prepare ourselves as she felt that Mammy had only a few hours left.

Dr Forde came downstairs at around 12.45 pm – normally I would have been eager to hear what he thought – instead I left him with Dominic, Anne and Liam and I went upstairs to Mammy.

When I got into her room, I felt a cold wind blow through the open window. I went over to close it and noticed that Mammy's breathing was so quiet and shallow now. I turned to look at her and noticed a frighteningly grey pallor on her face – I knew this was it.

I kicked the floor with my heel for the others to come and they raced up.

Anne was first in the door and I said to her: "She's going Anne."

Anne fell to her knees beside Mammy and begged her not to go. From somewhere I managed to say to Anne: "Let her go Anne – her pain is nearly over now."

I held Mammy's left hand, Anne was gently rubbing her arm, Dominic's face rested on Mammy's forehead and Liam held her right hand. Her four precious children all around her – one loved no more strongly than the other. Mammy then opened her eyes and looked around the room before slowly closing them again.

At eight minutes past one, on that sunny Sunday afternoon, my help, my greatest friend, my confidante, my very reason for living, slipped very, very peacefully away.

Dr Forde sat very quietly at the back of the room.

I knew the very second she died. I didn't need him to confirm it but when he did, the four of us convulsed into a flood of tears.

She was gone.

All the thoughts, all the memories came flooding back in that moment. I knew instantly that my life was never going to be the same again. It was as if a vital muscle to my heart had been removed – I felt incomplete. And in a way I was because it was Mammy who made me complete.

The task now was to live on without her. That would be the greatest gift I could give her. But just in that moment, I wondered just how the hell I was going to do it.

NINE

THE ULTIMATE GRIEF

We decided to have the funeral a couple of days later. As Mammy had wanted, she would stay in the house until her removal to the church. I thought I would be more emotional when the undertakers brought her back to us on the Sunday night. I thought that seeing her in a coffin would destroy me. Yet when I saw her body I didn't cry. In truth, it didn't look like Mammy.

It was all just so surreal. Here was the woman who my life had revolved around for as long as my memory could recall, now gone from me – unable to communicate ever again.

As the hours passed, it became clearer in my head and in my heart that this was indeed Mammy. There she was, in her favourite place in the sitting-room, where she sometimes dozed while reading or latterly while listening to the radio. Now she was sleeping one last time in that place.

Very early on the Monday morning, while everyone was asleep upstairs, I took out the breakfast things, made myself a cup of tea, sat beside the coffin and for the last time had breakfast with Mammy. I used to love these times that I shared with her and I was determined to have, if not enjoy, this one last meal together. I sat there, with my hand resting on her cold forehead, telling her things that I should really have told her when she was alive, but yet things that I knew she knew anyway, simply summed up in the words "Thanks" and "I love you".

Mammy's friends came in during the day to say their goodbyes to her and the sitting-room quickly became packed. When we were getting ready to bring Mammy on her last journey to the church, I told Dominic that I wanted just a few moments alone with her, to say my last goodbye before the undertakers took charge.

And so it happened.

I'd vowed that I would be strong, strangely just for her and that I would just kiss her and say goodbye. I had almost achieved this, when as I touched her lovely face for the very last time, I became hysterical – there is no other way to describe it. I just remember saying "Sorry" to her over and over again. Initially I was saying sorry for not keeping myself composed, as I'd hoped I would. I knew that Dominic, Anne and Liam were suffering as much as I was and I did not want to increase their pain by losing it. But I knew that in those last ever moments that I was going to have with her, I really needed to tell her how sorry I was for all the hassle, all the worry, all the fears and heartache, that I had brought to her life.

I knew that this really was the end and the realisation

of that was just too much for me to take. I managed somehow to tear myself away from her. When I got outside, for the first time in my life, I became so light-headed that I nearly fainted. I just grabbed hold of my cousin, Breda, in time.

I have faced many crises in my life, many moments when I felt utterly desolate and alone, yet that moment when I had to say goodbye to Mammy eclipsed them all. The short drive to the church was a journey that I had always dreaded having to take, as I knew that Mammy wasn't going to be with me.

The Removal went as well as these things can go. As requested by her, Liam and Fionn stood holding candles at the head of Mammy's coffin. Without doubt, my terrible sadness was helped by the sheer pride that I felt for the two lads that evening.

Tuesday, August 31, arrived. The day that I feared having to face more than any other day, was here. And much as I wanted to, I could not run away from it. Weather wise, it was a beautiful day. It was so different to the day of my father's funeral in 1986 when we were in the middle of Hurricane Charlie.

There is an awful finality on the funeral day of a loved one. When you see the mourning coach outside, waiting to bring the family to the Church for the final farewell, you would love to say to undertakers: "It's okay, we've changed our minds – everything's fine now."

But you know that everything is anything but fine.

The opening hymn of the Mass – 'Here I am Lord' – rang out: 'Here I am Lord, It is I Lord, I have heard you calling in the night.'

The Parish Priest, Fr Seamus (again Mammy's choice), commented after the hymn that he had never heard it sung so loudly by a congregation. I was secretly chuffed.

The Mass went by very quickly and, bizarrely, given the horror behind its intention, I actually liked it. I think it was the way Fr Seamus talked about Mammy throughout the mass in such glowing terms. My heart was bursting with pride. Lest there be anyone who didn't know as I did just what an incredible woman my mother was, people who knew her, some well and some not so well, and some who had never even met her, were hearing in a public place just how great my Ma was. This was really shown to me after the Mass, when people came over to express their sympathy. A friend of mine from work said: "Your mother sounded like a really lovely woman."

Mammy had always loved Sean Dunphy singing 'Pal of my Cradle Days'. For her birthday on St Valentine's Day 2003, I had gotten this played for her on Ronan Collins radio programme. She tried to make out I was "a big eejit," but I knew that she was pleased. So I'd asked the singers at the funeral, Matt and Catherine (who in 2005 became the Lord Mayor of Dublin), to sing this song at the Mass. It was self-indulgent, I know, but it was my way of telling everyone what Mammy had done for me, often at great personal sacrifice to herself. The entire song echoed around the silent congregation in the church. It was the one stage of the mass where I was utterly, totally, uncontrollably overcome, absolutely bereft.

But those words Ma are for you. They are as true now as they were in all our struggles together, when giving up on me could have been an option for you to take. And I say it with all my heart, if you had taken that option I would not have blamed you. But I do not believe that you ever considered it for a second...

> *Dearest Friend, Greatest Pal*
> *It was me who caused you*
> *Every sorrow and heartache you knew.....*
> *Pal of My Cradle Days*
> *I needed you always*
> *Since I was a baby upon your knee*
> *You sacrificed everything for me...*

We then drove the couple of miles to Palmerstown Cemetery. I had driven that journey so many times with Mammy when we went up to my Da's grave every Saturday. Now it was no longer just his grave. For ever more it would be my parents' grave.

As I sat in the mourning coach at the graveyard, Anne came over to me and asked if I would like it if Mammy was carried to the graveside. Barely able to get the words out I said that I would. Fionn was standing beside her. Seeing my distress he placed his young hand on my arm and gripped it. It was a simple gesture which meant then, and still does, so much to me.

I stood well away from the grave. I just couldn't bear to see the coffin being lowered into the ground. I stood by myself, not lonely but very much alone.

I didn't cry. I felt numb. Exactly 42 years to the day since she gave birth to me, I stood there knowing that my dearest friend, my greatest pal, was gone.

* * * *

After the funeral we went to the West County Hotel in Chapelizod for a meal. I've always thought that this 'tradition' of doing something like that after a funeral was a little inappropriate. But that day changed my thinking.

It was somehow right that we didn't just go away from the graveside, left with our individual thoughts and sadness. God knows there would be plenty of time to do that in the days, weeks and months ahead. But just in the immediate aftermath of the funeral it was good that as a family, and with our extended family and friends, we could be together, to talk about and think fondly of Mammy. It was a help to not be afraid to say just how much we were all going to miss her.

We eventually left mid-afternoon. The four of us went back to our family home, the home that our mother was never to be physically in again. That thought began to really traumatise me, so that evening I went up to Finnstown House in Lucan with my cousin, Breda.

We sat in the grounds for about half an hour, just talking about my Ma. The sun was beating down and I noticed that the knot of fear and worry in my stomach was gone. It suddenly dawned on me that I had spent so many years of my life worrying that something bad might happen to Mammy. And here I was, my fears ultimately fulfilled and I would have given anything to have that knot of fear back. And then I wondered did Mammy have that same knot of fear worrying about me. Of course she did. And in my desperation to find brightness, I consoled myself that at least we were both freed from worrying about each other. But God was it a poor consolation.

The first few days following the funeral were a blur. It felt strange, firstly getting used to the fact that she was gone, and, secondly, and weirdly, not doing the things that over the previous few weeks had become my routine. It was odd not to be giving Mammy her medication, preparing meals for her, feeding her, and just sitting with her. There was a sense of freedom which I felt so guilty for feeling.

It was a freedom that I would have given up gladly.

I knew that I could not be in the house on the first Sunday after Mammy died. I had always loved our Sundays together although surprisingly none stand out in my memory. I just have the knowledge, with the benefit of hindsight, of how special those times were, that I maybe took them for granted, and that I will never experience those days again. Even though sickness had temporarily ended our Sundays together, death had now permanently done so. And yet that first Sunday I did not want to be with anyone. I wanted more than ever to be by myself. So I drove to Donegal on the Sunday morning after Mammy died.

The stereo in the car went on the blink before the journey so I had no music, no talk, to distract me on the long journey to Letterkenny. I was alone with my thoughts and memories. I also had that awful empty feeling in the pit of my stomach. It is that emptiness which starts in your stomach, feels like it has a life of its own and spreads throughout your entire body until you feel that you are completely immersed in emptiness.

I drove many miles through the wilds of Donegal over the next few days, trying to replace the air of sorrow I was breathing with an oxygen of hope. The weather was lovely. I remember getting out of the car in one completely deserted area. There were hills and fields all around, total silence only broken by the odd sheep or a car passing by very infrequently. I stood at the side of the car, breathing in huge gulps of fresh air. And then the horrible realisation came crashing back – that no matter where I ran to, no matter how remote the place was that I travelled to, Mammy was gone and was never, ever coming back.

I slumped to the ground, sobbing. It was the

culmination of all the previous months sorrow wrapped up together and flooding out on that remote countryside spot. And right then I didn't want to be alone anymore. I desperately wanted someone to take me in their arms and say that it would be alright, that I was not alone. The curative properties of a simple hug are so great and how I could have done with one then!

I stayed in Donegal for a couple of days until I realised that I had to stop running away. I had to go home to try to pick up the pieces. Whereas before when I was away, I would try to get home by the quickest route, now my reason for doing that was gone, so I took the longest way home.

I drove through Tyrone, up to Belfast, just trying to put off the inevitable for as long as I possibly could.

I arrived home around 8 o'clock on the Wednesday evening. It was ten days since Mammy had died. As by this stage, Dominic, Anne and Liam had all returned home to their now changed lives without Mammy, this was the first time that I had put the key in the door to the house that I was now to live in alone. It was tough then, as it still is. But that awful, hollow pain of loss does lessen. It never, ever goes away though. People say at times of bereavement that "time will heal" by way of trying to comfort. I know that when people said this to me I just wanted to tell them to piss off, that you could never envisage this feeling of emptiness ever leaving you. But people mean well and death does turn the most eloquent into incoherent fools as you feel so desperate to console but realise that words are so inadequate.

I had bereavement counselling. It is recommended that if counselling is required it should begin a few months after the death of a loved one. The Hospice are so good to the families of the bereaved. They don't consider their work to be done when the patient they have been caring for has passed away. They follow up with the family for a time afterwards and, in fact, a couple of weeks after Mammy died, Karen from the Hospice rang me to see how I was getting on. Apparently, she got something of a shock at how distressed I was so she arranged for counselling to begin straightaway. I would so highly recommend this for anyone who has lost someone whom they loved and feel so lost without.

My counsellor, Neil, was simply incredible. Initially, hardly a session went by without the majority of it being spent with me just crying. My heart was simply broken at the loss of my Ma. Gradually, Neil sought to help me see that I had to plot a different course now, without my Ma. This resulted in my losing my temper with him on a couple of occasions. When we later spoke about this, he recalled one particular time when he'd thought I might hit him! This came about when he asked me: "Do you ever see the day when you will find that you are used to life without your mother?"

And I do remember feeling furious with him. How the hell was I ever going to, or more accurately want to, be used to life without Mammy. And yet Neil was so right. He was gently introducing the notion that one day, maybe without me even knowing it, my life would become different now that my Ma was no longer in it. And that, I believe, is what bereavement counselling is aimed at – to bring the grieving person to see, no matter how hard they try not to, that their loved one is gone and is never coming back.

In essence, I felt that bereavement counselling helped me in two crucial ways. Firstly, it validated my feelings of misery – of feeling totally and utterly crap; of getting no enjoyment from anything; of wishing, wishing, constantly wishing, that the person that I had lost was back with me again. It helped me to realise that I was perfectly entitled to feel that way. Secondly, it helped me to chart a course for the future; to make some sense of a future which at the time of my loss seemed so utterly bleak.

Losing someone you love through death confuses the clearest thinking mind. You are not responsible for your thoughts which, at times, can be crazily irrational. Soon after Mammy died, a well meaning person suggested that I should sort out Mammy's clothes and give them to charity. And, irrationally, I thought that there was no way I could do this – not because I needed to keep them to remind me of her but because a part of me still clung on to the hope that Mammy might come back and would need them when she did.

When I said this to Neil he said that this was a perfectly normal reaction. He explained that there was no time limit on when I would deal with her clothes and that I would do it when I was ready. And I did, but it took me a long, long time and I only did it when I felt that I was 100 per cent ready to do so. I did it with Anne's help and I think sharing the task helped both of us.

And you also do the strangest things after you lose someone you've loved so much. For instance, for months afterwards, when I was making myself a cup of tea, I would ask aloud: "Want a cup of tea Ma?"

It was just so that I could hear those words that I had spoken so many times before again.

Or when I was leaving for work in the morning, I would still shout up the stairs as I had done for so many years: "I'm going Ma."

And I would always wait a few seconds, in the vain hope that I would hear her reply back to me: "See ya Ger, mind them roads," as she had done every morning of my working life.

For a long time, bizarre as it may sound, when I was in work I would still ring home every day, praying that she would answer with her usual greeting when she knew it was me: "Ah there you are Ger."

And for such a long time, every evening when I came home from work and went into the sitting room, I turned to look at the chair that she sat in. I was hoping against hope that this had all been just an awful dream and that she would be back sitting there.

And no matter how hard I prayed for it, I knew that it was a prayer that would never be answered. I remember saying to Neil that I would give away everything, every cent, every possession I owned if I could just sit and have a cup of tea with my Ma one last time. And yet my faith is so childlike that I truly, firmly believe that one day we will meet again. That there is a Heaven where all sorrow and heartache will be gone, where we will be together again forever. If I did not believe that I would be in total despair. In my head it's as if it will be like some grand railway station where, when my life is over, Mammy will be there waiting to welcome me home. It's why I now would never fear dying – it's why, I'm sure, that Mammy did not fear dying.

But no matter how much counselling you seek or receive or how many books you read on dealing with grief and loss or how you try to re-build your life, when you lose someone whom you love so deeply, that wound will never, ever fully heal. That pain of loss will never fully go away; that piece of your heart is gone forever.

The emptiness in your life that their absence has brought about can never, ever be filled. The pleasures which you had in life no longer give you the same pleasure as they did before. Life is so completely different. You just have to try to accept that difference and accommodate it in your changed life.

Grief is such an insidious and unwelcome visitor into your life. It can make you selfish in that you are so focussed on just concentrating on pulling yourself through it. I know that the other three worried about me – knowing the bond that Mammy and I had and also that I was now living alone in the family house. And yet I wanted them to deal with their own grief. She was their mother just as much as she was mine – her loss was felt by them as much as I was feeling it. And maybe, in a strange way, worrying about me helped them. I hope it did. And we definitely became closer. Surely there can be no greater epitaph to a parent or parents than that.

Somehow, the first Christmas without Mammy came round, despite my incredible desire for it not to. I decided to launch headlong into it – to try to enjoy it rather than feel miserable because of it. I made my first Christmas pudding (which was an overwhelming success!) and cooked Christmas dinner for Anne and the three kids, Dominic and myself. With a guiding hand from on high, I'm sure, it was a great success and, if I'm honest, was a very enjoyable Christmas.

I couldn't believe that for the first time in my life, I had cooked a full Christmas dinner by myself. From spiced beef, turkey, ham, stuffing (which I made myself - none of this store bought stuff!) to me even pushing the boat out and making special stuffing for Anne as she is a coeliac, you name it – we had it! I hoped that no one would get maudlin as I knew it would only set me off. But Anne hit the perfect note. When the dinner was ready and we all sat down to eat, she placed a candle in the middle of the table, lit it and said: "This is just to remember those who can't be here."

Simple, perfect and hit the spot.

Of course there were various times during the day when one of us was swept up on a wave of melancholia but it was not as horrendous as I had anticipated and I was so pleased that I managed not to go on a guilt-trip about that.

After the Christmas buzz that first winter was really tough. The combination of getting up for work when the mornings were really dark and coming home from work on shadowy evenings can give you the blues at the best of times and clearly these were not the best of times. In fact the mornings and the evenings described my mood perfectly, DARK. I was dark and so lonely without Mammy.

The functionary things that you have to do after somebody dies only served to magnify my sadness. Things like cancelling her pension, sorting out her Life Insurance, closing credit union and bank accounts. God love her, she didn't have a lot in these accounts and this only made me feel even sadder. I hated changing everything to do with the house into my name, as this would mean that all future correspondence on this would be addressed to me rather than to her. Instead of feeling horrible when mail arrived for her, it had the opposite effect on me. It perpetuated the thought in my head that although she was gone she would be back, as if she had only gone on an extended holiday. Gradually, I began to realise that this was an impossible dream and slowly I did start to change things into my name. But the feeling of total betrayal I felt was horrible.

The first few days, weeks and months after you lose someone as close to you as Mammy was to me, are purely and simply a matter of punching time and hoping that you scrape through it. That was the sum total of my ambition and slowly, very slowly, the horrible darkness began to lift. A glimmer of light began to shine through. I know that some people were astounded that I hadn't folded like a pack of cards when Mammy died, and if I'm honest I was one of them! I was determined not to though. I felt that if I did I would be in some ways betraying her memory and all that she had striven for to give me the best life possible.

At the same time, there were some really awful days. Two particularly spring to mind. The first was on her birthday, St Valentines Day, February 14, 2005, after she had died, I really struggled through that day. Maybe it is the symbolism of having a birthday fall on St Valentine's Day. It always used to make me smile when I was in card shops around that date. Other people would be hunting for their particular choice of Valentine's cards, while I would be getting Mammy's birthday card. She was very traditional in that she was never very keen on funny cards. She definitely preferred ones with a nice verse! Now that was alright when she was able to read them herself. But as her sight deteriorated so rapidly in her final years, you then had to read the verses out for her. This was always very difficult as I, soppy fool that I was, (and very much still am!) would always choke up reading the verses for her. But God, how I wished that I needed to buy her a card that day and that I could read her the soppy verse. The realisation that I couldn't, nor would I ever be able to again, just floored me. Instead I bought flowers for the grave. As I was buying them, the shop assistant, obviously assuming that I was buying them for a wife or girlfriend, said: "She's a lucky lady – she'll love them."

What could I say?

As I placed the flowers on the grave, I was completely bereft. 'This is so wrong,' I kept thinking. Visits to the grave since the funeral had normally resulted in my breaking down but that day was ten times, a hundred times, as many times as you care to mention, worse. The pain of loss felt as bad that day as it had six months previously. As a family, we all did our own thing on the day, marking it in our own way. Each one of us was probably fearful, as I was, that if we had done anything together the emotion of it would probably just have been too overwhelming.

The second terrible day was when my Ma's old neighbour and friend, Tommy Byrne, died in April 2005. I went to his funeral which was in the same church as Mammy's. The same priest had celebrated the Mass, on that sunny day, eight months previously. Without anticipating it, Tommy's funeral took so much out of me – the memories came flooding back, not that they had ever gone away in the first place. And yet, undoubtedly with the benefit of the ongoing bereavement counselling, I knew that this was all part of the grieving process. I knew that there were going to be many such mountains to climb before I could find some sort of peace. And I realise now that it is so vital that you do not run away from such crisis points. You cannot run away or hide from your grief. You have to allow it time to live, to manifest itself in whatever way it will. You have to face it head-on, slug it out with it and just hope against hope that you are still standing at the end of the tussle.

It's a damned hard fight. But as sure as night follows

day, it is a fight that we will all have to face at some stage in our lives. The pain of loss never goes away. It just gets less acute perhaps, but it never goes away. I know that even now, over four years since Mammy died. I still feel so lost at times. And in a way that is the best way to describe how I am without Mammy – I am utterly lost without her. Not for the functionary things such as cooking, shopping, ironing and the rest, as I was always, to a great extent, independent of her for such things. My loss is the sheer companionship, the empathy and the joy of living with someone who loved you for all your ups and many downs and who knew just how to help you cope with the trials of life.

But, as I say, the acute pain does lessen. There is no panacea for this pain. Just punch the time, use whatever back-up resources that are available and hope and pray that the darkness will give way to some form of light. It is foolish to expect it to be a glowing light for that glowing light has been extinguished and can't ever return again.

TEN

AN UNWELCOME BREAK

'Murphy's Law' is such that at times of bereavement you feel that everything else in your life has also taken a wrong turn and that you are constantly battling against adversity. Only on these occasions I hadn't gotten my battle partner to help me through. And by God this became so evident to me on the night of Thursday, June 23, 2005, less than ten months after losing Mammy.

I had begun to see life a little bit more clearly. Work didn't inspire me in the least. I had applied for a new job outside the Civil Service some weeks previously, was unsuccessful after having been short-listed for the position but was not unduly bothered.

I'd also decided to head off by myself for a few days to Cork and Kerry. I wanted to go by myself because a couple of weeks previously I had rung a friend of mine, not really for anything in particular, basically just to shoot the breeze. His reaction at the end of our chat spooked me when he said: "Do you realise that we have gotten through a conversation without you talking about your mother?"

The relief in his voice was palpable. Was I being a bit of a pain in the arse by talking about Mammy as much as I obviously was? It was just that I thought about her at every waking moment. I just missed her so incredibly. But I also realised that maybe it would be unfair to go away with anyone as my feelings were still just so raw. I knew that the topic of conversation would invariably revolve around my Ma.

So off I'd gone and driving around the Ring of Kerry, I'd actually found myself singing along to a song on the radio, as if I hadn't a care in the world. I remember stopping and instead of reproaching myself, as I would have expected, instead I was so pleased that I was in a state which although it could certainly not be described as happiness, was not the all consuming state of sadness which had been my life during Mammy's illness and particularly after she died. I was so glad and I knew that Mammy would be too. I'd gone back to work on Thursday, June 23, fairly happy, fairly content and not totally dreading the future. I was happy to let it unfold as it would, but that's when fate took a serious hand in proceedings.

That first day back in work, after three weeks holidays, was utterly uneventful – the summer lull really in place. I locked up the house that night, put the alarm on as usual and was getting ready to relax in bed watching 'The West Wing' on TV. I had gone into the bathroom just as the advertisements were on before the programme. As I was coming out, I heard the familiar drum-roll of the theme music. I rushed out of the half-opened sliding door and in my haste I kicked the bottom of the door with my right foot. I felt myself beginning to stumble. I wasn't sure if I was actually going to fall – I thought that maybe I could regain my balance. Then I realised in the next split-second that the locker just outside the bathroom door was directly in my flight-path. If I fell on that I was in danger of whacking my head off it or of smashing my teeth, thus destroying my rugged good looks! So in mid-air, I somehow managed to manoeuvre myself to avoid the locker but in doing so I landed full-force on the floor.

Now as any disabled person will testify falls are an occupational hazard. You just hope that they don't happen in a public place where the pain of embarrassment is much worse than any physical pain which might ensue. This time when I hit the floor, I heard an unmerciful crack, like someone snapping a plank of wood. My first thought was 'Shit, I've broken the locker'. However in that rush of thoughts I wondered how I could have done that since I had fallen so far away from it. Then a searing pain, unlike any I had experienced before in my life, shot through my left arm. I didn't know where my arm actually was – it wasn't under me – it was as if it was separated from me. I looked behind me and my arm seemed to be an inordinate distance away from me, back on the bathroom floor. I was convinced that, somehow, I had severed it from the rest of my body as I noticed that it was quivering yet I wasn't moving it.

I literally started to crawl back to my arm, thinking I should gather it back into my body. Even that simple act caused such massive pain. Now if you were to fold a pair of socks into one and then swing them around in a lasso movement, then that is exactly how my arm was acting. When I gathered it back in to me, it seemed to have an uncontrollable life of its own, swinging around at all sorts of strange angles while I tried desperately to hold it still. The more it swung the more pain I was in.

I knew instantly that I had broken it, and broken it badly. And yet, the incredible pain of the break was quickly replaced by thoughts of what the hell this was going to mean. To walk, I required both arms for balance purposes – you don't see too many tightrope walkers doing their gig with one arm tied behind their back do you? I knew, even through the unbelievable pain I was in, that this was the beginning of a seriously bad time which was going to have huge long-term consequences for me.

I gave serious thought to trying to get into bed, hoping that it would be better in the morning. I quickly realised that this was not an option. This was not something that I could pretend had not happened – I was in serious trouble here.

I crawled to the phone and rang Liam who lives a couple of miles away. I knew that if I rang 999 that the doors would have to be knocked down as I just could not get to them, so, as Liam had a key to the house he was my best option. Liam, and his young lad, Liam Jnr, arrived very quickly and rang for an ambulance.

While I was waiting for Liam to arrive and then while we were waiting for the ambulance, I sat there holding my smashed arm to me, as each time I let it go it flopped every which way. I sat there in awful pain, yet my mind was not focused on the pain but on the consequences of my accident.

To get to the phone I had crawled to such an awkward position that when the ambulance men arrived and tried to get me onto a stretcher I was screaming in agony. Given my existing spinal difficulties, they were really concerned that I might have done some further spinal damage in the fall, especially as even the slightest movement caused me such distress. They decided to call in the Fire Brigade. As they didn't have a spinal board with them, they asked the Fire Brigade to bring one so that they could extricate me from the position I'd gotten myself into without causing any further damage.

When they arrived, the room was very quickly filled with men, each taking hold of a piece of me and placing me very gently onto the spinal board and then onto the stretcher.

I remember being wheeled from the house to the ambulance and staring up at the post-midnight sky. The flashing lights of the ambulance and the fire brigade were illuminating it. In that moment I just knew that people who were watching this scene would immediately put two and two together and come up with five. I was sure they would assume that I was lost without my mother and that I had tried to do "something silly" in my loneliness. I felt this overwhelming urge to shout out that it was an accident and then thought that maybe they would have felt: "he doth protest too much!" So I was carted off with speculation, no doubt, at fever pitch.

One thing is sure though, Ballyfermot, like most predominately working-class areas, has its critics, but the neighbours you have there will be difficult to find anywhere else. I found this to be particularly so after Mammy died. They seemed to take an extra few seconds to say hello to me, as if to reassure themselves that I was doing okay. So when they heard about my accident the next day, the shock of it must have given credence to the fears people had that I would struggle without her. But, in truth, the accident could so easily have happened if Mammy had still been alive. Thankfully it never did. In that rush of pain and fear that I experienced that night, I do remember clearly thinking, 'What the hell would I have done if this had happened last year when Mammy was sick?' That horror scenario chilled me.

The journey to the hospital was tortuous – sirens blaring, lights flashing, every ramp and pothole on the way being hit and sending further surges of pain through me. I asked the ambulance men what hospital they were taking me to, praying that they wouldn't say St James's. It held too many horrible memories for me and I just didn't need to add to them. But, of course, they replied: "St James's."

When we got to the Accident and Emergency Department, I begged the ambulance men to be careful bringing me into the hospital as I was just about at the end of my pain threshold. They nearly succeeded until they cut a corner, pushing me through the door of the hospital, smacking my arm against it. I should have known that I was well within the grip of Sod's Law then.

My arm was X-rayed straight away. It is incredible how staff in A&E Units assume that a fall late at night by a non-elderly person is automatically drink or drugs related. I knew by the tone of some of the staff that that was the assumption they had made about me. And in a way who can blame them as I'm sure they see so many such instances. A noticeable change occurred when I informed them that I didn't, in fact, drink. How good it felt saying that at such an otherwise awful time.

I had foolishly and incredibly naively asked one of the nurses if he thought I would have to stay in hospital. He said they wouldn't be able to say until they saw the X-ray.

When it arrived the X-ray showed that my humerus bone was broken in four places, "shattered" was the word that one doctor used to describe it. The humerus must be the most inappropriately named bone in the human body given the months of misery that it was about to bring me. When I was shown the X-ray I knew that I was in deep shit as the bone looked as if someone had been at it with a hatchet.

The nurse's reaction on seeing the X-ray confirmed my worst fears.

"Tá se briste mór," he said, as if by speaking our native tongue the blow might be cushioned slightly.

It wasn't.

When Liam came into the cubicle in the A&E Unit his face dropped. My blood oxygen levels were really low due to the shock of the accident so I was wearing an oxygen mask to try to replenish. My arm was completely covered in Plaster of Paris and was resting on a pillow. My shirt had been cut off when I arrived at the hospital and the remainder of it was still hanging off my right side.

I remember mumbling to him through the mask: "I'm alright."

But if he could have read my mind he would have seen me pondering upon the horror which I just knew was to come in the weeks and months ahead.

I almost begged the doctors on duty to operate to fix

it, knowing that this would be the quickest way for me to get back to normal. However, the consultant decided that conservative management was the best approach to take. He felt that surgery ran too great a risk of causing nerve damage in my arm which would, he informed me, have rendered it useless for life. That prospect scared the life out of me as to all intents and purposes that would have left me not far off quadriplegia. As the doctor on duty in the A&E Unit said so succinctly on seeing my X-ray, and taking my disability into consideration: "Do you realise that you are one break away from being Christopher Reeve?"

Okay, his bedside manner may have left a lot to be desired and he may have been gilding the lily slightly, but the basic tenet of his argument was undeniable and very frightening.

There followed a week in St James's which was almost too cruel for words – being wheeled up and down corridors which barely a year before I had walked so many times on my way to visit Mammy. I had hoped that I would never have had to step foot inside the place again – to have to do so that soon and with something which I just knew was going to have such a detrimental effect on my independent life, was so cruel.

I lost count of the amount of times I asked for the arm to be surgically fixed. On each occasion I was met by a stone wall: "Trust us, we know best."

During that week one of the night nurses on duty said to me after a couple of days: "Would you mind if I suggested that you be referred to the hospital's Psychiatry Team?"

I was a bit taken aback and asked why she was suggesting it. She said that over the couple of days since

I had been admitted, I just seemed more and more down each time she saw me.

"It's been a long time since I remember seeing anyone so sad," she said, genuinely concerned.

I agreed to the referral as I knew that I was at an incredibly, low ebb.

The next day the psychiatrist and her team of around half a dozen junior doctors arrived at my bedside and asked if I would like to talk.

I said I would, so they pulled the curtain around the bed. Why do doctors and hospital staff generally have this idea that if you pull this flimsy curtain around a patient's bed, that you are suddenly cocooned in some soundproof bubble!

But in truth I didn't care who heard. I proceeded to tell them about Mammy, her illness, her death, how I had been since then and everything I just knew that my accident was going to bring into my life.

One of the junior doctors asked, perhaps a little bluntly but hopefully not in a suggestive way: "Have you given any consideration into taking your own life over the last few days?"

Incredibly, from somewhere I laughed and said to him: "For fuck sake, will you look at me. My left arm is in plaster, from my fingers to my shoulder. I have Spina Bifida so I can't walk without callipers and I can't get at them. Even if I could I would need someone to help me put them on now, so I'm stuck here. So unless I try to poke myself to death with my right hand, it looks like I just might have to tough this one out."

Okay, so it's not one of the great stand-up routines (if you know what I mean!) but I at least expected someone to break ranks and snigger. Instead they all lowered their heads in a sympathetic way, said nothing, but their collective expressions just screamed at me: "You poor bastard."

The psychiatrist said that they would keep an eye on me but that she wouldn't prescribe any medication. She asked if I would see them again in two weeks time. As I wasn't anticipating any pressing engagements, I agreed to do so. When I returned a couple of weeks later for my follow-up visit, they suggested that I go on anti-depressants. Given my track record, the prospect of potentially developing another addiction made me knock that idea on the head pretty quickly.

At the end of the week in St James's, I knew in my heart that I could not go home to my own house. My balance was so compromised – mere toilet visits were an ordeal. The simple act of achieving an independently managed bowel movement became my total focus of attention. All the support bars in the hospital were on my left side, my broken arm side (Good old Sod's Law again!). So during that week I was forced into using a commode. Even the name smacks of someone who is totally dependent on others, unable even to go to the toilet themselves. And here I was now – thrust into that very position.

The first time I used it was late on an extremely hot and balmy night, in late June. Despite windows being opened and the liberal use of air fresheners, I was so conscious of the smell that this most natural act had caused. The indignity of being helped back to bed when I was finished, while the commode was wheeled away, just seemed to add to the horror. Once back in bed, sleep was the last thing that I felt like doing. I just lay there hating myself for being so dependant and cursing God for putting me through this.

The next time I needed to use it I stayed awake all night, until around 4 am, when I hoped that the other patients in the ward would be asleep. Even the act of getting out of bed without callipers, with one arm weighed down by injury and Plaster of Paris, was such a struggle. When I eventually got myself onto it, I sat there beside the opened window, curtains closed, begging my bowels to move quickly and quietly. I rested my head on my good arm on the window sill and wept. My dignity was gone. My independence, which Mammy had fought to attain, and I had striven to maintain and sustain was gone. In essence, I was now the person that that doctor had predicted I would be to Mammy all those years previously – and all because of a broken arm.

It was as if the broken arm had removed a veil of secrecy that had lain over my disability. For the first time what had been in many ways a hidden intense physical vulnerability was now exposed. It had a vice-like grip on me and realistically there wasn't a damned thing I could do about it. I just had to accept that for the foreseeable future I was going to have to depend on others for everything, from having a shower to having a crap. The horror of this realisation and the speed at which it had happened in my life terrified me. I remember saying to my family, with the benefit of hindsight unfairly, that if the nurses brought around the medication and put a tablet in front of me saying, "Whatever you do, don't take that tablet or you will die", I know, without any hesitation or consideration, that I would have taken that tablet. For at that stage I just knew that this wasn't going to be just a couple of weeks of inconvenience. This was going to be a long, long haul and I really felt that maybe this was just a bridge too far, a hurdle too high, for me to climb.

When the medical staff recommended that I go to the Orthopaedic Hospital in Clontarf, again negative perceptions came forth. In my head it was a home for the elderly, a home for those unable to look after themselves – a HOME. And not home in the sense of a place of safety and warmth on a wet, cold Monday night in winter. This was home with every negative connotation you could imagine. I felt it was to be my incarceration.

On Wednesday, June 29, I was transferred by ambulance to Clontarf. All my preconceived ideas about the place were confirmed immediately upon my arrival. There were so many elderly people there, who I initially saw as occupants of God's waiting room. But as the days and weeks passed, I realised they were as anxious to get well and return to their own homes as I was. In many ways, they were all in a better position than me, as they had all had surgery and were undergoing physiotherapy to achieve the goal of getting home. I was unable to do physio, however, as my arm was to remain immobilised, so I was basically just being looked after. The dawning of that realisation hit me so quickly and resulted in my sense of despair growing intensely.

That first evening in Clontarf was, without doubt, the lowest ebb of my life. There had been many low ebbs before, some so very recently but this absolutely was the worst. The feeling of utter helplessness, the feeling of almost being imprisoned for a crime I hadn't committed, was awful. Dominic, Anne and Liam came to see me that evening and I knew by the looks on their faces that they were so worried about me. Never had they seen me in such despair. I had missed Mammy so much since she died but here I was now needing her more than ever, needing HER to tell me that everything was going to be alright. And the fact that she wasn't there to do so, nor ever would be again, just seemed to compound my misery.

Each of them tried to make me see that things wouldn't always be this bad. They said that as soon as my arm was fixed I would be back to normal. I tried to explain how I just knew that this was going to have such a long-term negative effect on me but, possibly because they were so desperate for me not to focus on the bleak they didn't seem to fully realise that this was a Rubicon in my life. And yet in the midst of my misery, I felt the solidarity of the four of us being there together. When they were getting ready to leave, I so desperately wanted to ask them to stay as I just did not want to be alone. But in a way it was good that they did leave, as I knew that I would have to adjust to my 'imprisonment' pretty quickly.

The next morning, the consultant from St James's came to the hospital in Clontarf to check up on the couple of patients who were there under his care. A friend of mine, Joe Duffy, had called in to see me on his way to work in RTE. Joe was obviously concerned at how low I was and when the consultant came to me, Joe said to him: "Would you not operate to fix his arm? He's in a really bad way here."

And not for the first or the last time, the consultant said that conservative management was best and that he knew what he was doing.

There was nothing for either of us to say but I was grateful to Joe for trying. However, the consultant was not for turning.

My obsession with getting to the toilet by myself kicked in almost immediately. It was as though this was the benchmark I was using to gauge just how dependent I had become on others. It took a few days and I would be lying if I said that it was the independent act that it should be, but a compromise of sorts was found. There were many indignities along the way though.

The toilet which I found most convenient and user-friendly was on the main corridor where patients, visitors and the world and it's mother walked. The toilet drill which I developed was that an attendant, of which the Orthopaedic Hospital in Clontarf is blessed with so many incredible ones (Health Care Assistants to give them their proper title), would walk with me to the toilet. I tried to walk as much as possible, using a large walking frame. Trying to walk with a crutch, a stick, or linking somebody's arm was too risky because moving with my arm tied to me was impossible. If I did it I ran the risk of stumbling thus damaging the arm further, if that was possible.

Once we arrived at the toilet; I was then stuck, as I was only able to pull down one side of my trousers. So he would pull down the other side and then my boxers for me, make sure I was safely on the toilet and leave me to do the business. Fortunately, I was able to do my own ablutions after the deed was done, as that would just have been an indignity too far. Unfortunately though, when the attendant left the toilet, the door was out of my reach. I wasn't able to lock it so I used have to hold a chair against it, hoping that this would deter would be users of the convenience. One day, though, a persistent gentleman who was hard of hearing pushed the door so hard that I lost the grip I had on the chair. When he saw me sitting there he left but he didn't close the door after himself. I sat there for what seemed like ages, good hand covering the family jewels, trousers down around my ankles, as people walked by, looking in at me like some freak show or some weird modern day art exhibition. I asked God knows how many people to close the door until one man eventually obliged – from the inside, with him in the toilet with me! In a fairly unappreciative tone and language, I advised him that I wanted him to close the door from the outside. I can look back at it now and smile but at the time I was so pissed off (no pun intended) at what was just another blow to my self-image. Not alone was I disabled, but now I was in effect carrying a bloody great fluorescent sign around with me, proclaiming that I was disabled. It was all proving too much for me.

Just how I psychologically survived those first weeks in hospital, I'm not quite sure. But with the aid of friends and relations calling to see me, the staff in Clontarf, whom I could not speak highly enough about, and the fantastic sunshine that I enjoyed in the beautiful gardens of the hospital, I did survive. Although we love to complain about the weather, the summer of 2005 was one that nobody could moan about. I swear I was bronze when I was discharged after my five weeks there. Sitting in the sun for much of each day was probably not the cleverest thing to do from a medico/physical view but from a medico/ psychological perspective, it got me through. On the very rare days of inclement weather, boredom from reading newspapers or watching TV quickly set in.

My stay in Clontarf was the first time that the kids had ever seen me having to use a wheelchair. And, with the typical simplicity of children's minds they thought it was brilliant and envied me greatly! Fionn and Ellen got a great kick out of pushing me around the grounds at what was most assuredly a dangerous speed. They were more than a little miffed when I wouldn't get out of the chair to give them a go! They even joked that they would love to get a wheelchair for Christmas! God if only life was that simple.

So there were times during the stay when, I have to admit, that it wasn't totally horrific. When I was admitted to the hospital, I had immediately asked for a private room, thinking that if I was going to spend a long time there then I would prefer to be alone. As there were none available, I was placed on a public ward. A private room became available a few days later and after spending one night in it I asked to go back to the public ward. I couldn't stand the loneliness and isolation.

While on the public ward I met many patients. After a while I became one of the longest servers, as the turnover was amazing. Many were arriving immediately post-surgery, very immobile; many others after having hip or knee replacements; and all of them were then walking out, after an intensive time of physiotherapy and rehabilitation.

One patient who had been there for a long while when I arrived was Ben. He was around the same age as me and we were by some distance the youngest patients there. He had suffered horrific injuries in a motorbike accident. His grit and determination in the face of such obvious pain was awe inspiring. And yet one day he said to me that he admired how I was coping.

I was genuinely astonished and asked him what he meant.

"My injuries are bad," he said, "but they are healing. Although I'll probably never fully get back to how I was before my accident, even when your arm is fixed you'll still have your disability forever and yet you always seem so cheery. I really admire you."

How other people see us!

I was so sad when Ben was discharged. I was really happy for him, as by that stage he had spent months in hospital, but I was really sad that my buddy was going and I was staying.

And then there was this lovely old lady from Drimnagh, Mary. She had broken her leg while away abroad on holidays. While she was making a good recovery from the surgery to repair the damage, she was so fearful that the accident would be a precursor to losing her much valued independence. We had so many chats when I tried to reassure her that this was only a blip in her life and that she would soon be back to normal.

She told me that her husband had died many years previously.

"If only I was ten years older Mary, I'd be chasing after you," I used to say to her. "But you'd have to promise to walk very slowly so that I could catch you!"

We used to meet most evenings in the TV room, after the visitors had left. We'd try to encourage one another not to get too down-hearted at the misfortunes which had befallen us.

But there were also a few patients over the weeks I was in hospital who used to really piss me off, as I'm sure I did to some also. One guy in particular, we'll call him Dessie for purposes of discretion, was just too much. He knew everyone in the country personally and he also was an expert on any subject you cared to mention. One thing which used irritate me senseless was the way he always seemed to need the help of the female Health Care Assistants in putting his pyjamas on at night when it was obvious from his movements during the day that he was more than capable of performing this task himself. Need I be any more graphic?

At night the drill for us patients would be that we would each be issued with a urine bottle as pretty much all our mobility was limited and not exactly conducive to walking in and out of toilets in the dark. One night, Dessie woke everyone up, me included, from a deep slumber with his booming country accent shouting, or more accurately screaming: "Oh fuck, bollox, shite". A plethora of further expletives, too graphic to print, then followed in quick succession. The night staff ran in to find out what the commotion was and to see if he was alright.

"I'm after spilling that fucking piss bottle all over the bed, I'm fucking soaked," he bellowed.

Now how I didn't wet myself on hearing this, I'm not quite sure! I don't know if people wondered why I was sitting up in bed whispering up to the heavens above: "Thank you God!"

As time passed, I knew that I was not going to be discharged routinely from Clontarf – I had to make provision myself for my discharge. I had to put in place a strategy to prove to the powers that be in the hospital and also to myself, that my own home was the place that I should be in and that I was not putting myself at any risk by going back there.

I was due to return to the out-patients clinic in St James's on July 28, to see how the bone was progressing and to see if the conservative management of it was doing the trick. I had promised myself that if they considered that there had been any sort of an improvement, no matter how small, then I would go home. If not, then I would stay in Clontarf, knowing that although that decision would be made for the right physical reason, the psychological effect it would have on me would be very worrying. I knew that much as the care and attention which I received in Clontarf was second to none and a paradigm for how patients should be treated in a hospital setting, it was still, for the want of a better word, an institution. I was fully aware that the longer I stayed the more institutionalised I was becoming.

I began to make plans for my release from Clontarf as if I was Steve McQueen in 'The Great Escape'! Reluctantly I accepted that to have any chance of getting home, I would need a wheelchair, as I had become used, and yes safe, using one of the Hospital's chairs while in Clontarf. In my naivety, I thought that this would be a matter of contacting my local health service, telling them about my new, urgent circumstances and that they would quickly be able to provide me with one. But I'd forgotten that this is Ireland. When I enquired I was told that I would have to be assessed by a Health Board physiotherapist and that there was a waiting list for such an appointment. Then, if it was recommended that I should get a wheelchair, I would be placed on another waiting list for one. All told, the earliest I could expect to get one would be six months. So I made a few phone calls to private wheelchair sellers and eventually found a guy close to the Hospital who delivered a chair to me within a day. It cost me €200 but I was so determined to get home that I would have paid ten times that!

The news at the out-patient clinic was encouraging.
The bone appeared to be knitting and so I finalised my
arrangements to leave Clontarf the next day. The hospital
staff were reluctant, to say the least, to discharge me. It
took some persuasion on my part to convince them that
what I was doing was more aimed at my psychological well
being than anything else. In fairness to them, in their eyes I
was a person who would surely struggle to care for himself
at home. I knew the person that I was, though, and I knew
that if I couldn't do it I would not be afraid to ask for help.
Incredibly, despite the many times in Clontarf when I was
consumed with utter loneliness, sadness and downright
misery at the cards I had been dealt, I left the hospital on
that rainy Friday night with a heavy heart, filled with real
trepidation. For those who struggle to imagine how I was
feeling, think of how difficult your life would become if
suddenly you were left with no left leg and no left arm for,
to a massive extent, that is how I now was.

Dominic came to collect me that evening. I was
surprised by my reaction when he pushed me into the
sitting room of my house. I felt as if I had been away for
years, rather than weeks. I felt like a different person to the
one who had left the house by ambulance. And, in truth,
I was. I tried to hide the fact that I was overcome with
the emotion of it all from Dominic. He either sensed it,
or saw me and put his hand on my shoulder. What could
he say or do? In fairness, nothing.

It was a major shock to me when I woke up the
following morning in my own bed. Bizarrely, given how
determined I was to get out of the hospital, if somebody
had offered me the chance to go straight back to Clontarf,

then I would have taken it. I missed the security blanket that it shrouded me in. Dominic had moved in with me but I made it clear that unless I had independence, from a toileting and washing myself perspective, then I would not stay at home.

Before I set my escape plan in motion I had faced the fact that with my arm in plaster and unusable, and my balance compromised because of that, to ignore these problems would have merely been inviting another accident. So through a contact I had made in Clontarf, I had organised a rota of three Polish guys, Marcin, Marcin and Michal, with one of them to come every morning. They were to help me with everything. Literally the only thing I did was wipe my own arse. Everything else, from ensuring that I was safely on and off the toilet to washing, dressing and helping me put on the callipers, was done by the three lads. It is one thing to have to accept such help in hospital, to now have to accept it in my own home was such an indignity. Dominic had removed all clutter and installed grab rails in the toilet in anticipation of my return home which definitely made things a lot easier. This was just a sample of how good he was to me throughout the whole ordeal. I must have been a nightmare to be around during the months that followed, yet he soldiered on, seeming almost oblivious to my frustrations. If I live to be 100, I could not begin to thank him. His mother's son he most assuredly is.

The Polish lads were great. One of the Marcins had pretty good English but the other two lads struggled. They did assure me that I helped them enormously with the language. Michal worked in a bar and in the beginning was almost shy about speaking English. One day when he arrived he asked me how I was. Feeling particularly frustrated that day I said that being unable to do much was "driving me bananas". It took a little explaining to get across to him what that meant! However, a few weeks later he said that a stag party were in the bar the previous night and in a Polish accent it sounded so strange to hear him say: "They spend so much money and I am going to their table with drinks and food all night. Then when they leave they not even say thank you. That really drives me bananas."

I made the mistake of opening a bill one day when he was there, which was a lot more than I had anticipated it would be. I said: "If they think I'm paying that then they have their shite."

I tried so hard to explain this unique 'Dublinese' but failed!

Michal's English was really tested on one of the days that he came to me. My upper arm had been in the cast for about three months at this stage. On this particular morning, my lower arm and my hand had swollen to nearly twice their normal size. In truth, it looked like Popeye's arm after he'd had his fix of spinach! When Michal arrived, he got such a fright when he saw my arm that all his broken English well and truly escaped him and all he could say was: "Look, Look. Oh this is shit man!"

I rang the hospital and they suggested that I go to the plaster room in the hospital to make sure that the cast was not too tight. So myself and Michal headed off in a taxi to St James's. In the plaster room, while my arm was being re-cast, the difference in how two peoples' lives were lived really came home to me. In the cubicle next to mine, the Dublin Gaelic footballer Alan Brogan, was having a cast put on his leg. From what I could gather from ear-wigging, I think he had done some damage to his Achilles. After he had his cast put on, he was given a pair of crutches and told to come back in a few weeks. He hobbled away and, in fairness to him, he made no fuss at all. You would never have known that he was one of the finest players in the country, as he acted just like an ordinary patient. But I remember thinking that here we were, two people having casts put on for similar reasons of injury but whose lives were so vastly different. His, temporarily inconvenienced by injury, mine seemingly hurtling steadily downhill. How I wished we could change places!

One of the lads came every day for about two months until I realised that my soul was being destroyed by it. I decided that if I had another mishap then so be it but I was going to try to fend for myself for at least half of each week. It was traumatic and I had a lot of shaky moments. But around early October I did reach a time when I decided to try and go it alone.

Being a virtual prisoner at home was tough. In truth, I was unable to get out as my arm was in plaster, immobilised while they waited to see if it would fix by itself. I was also conscious of having to use the wheelchair which I needed help to manoeuvre. With only one working arm, if I pushed myself in it I would just go around in a circle! I virtually hadn't walked since coming home from Clontarf and I feared having another fall. The consequences of that were too awful to contemplate. 'What if I fell and broke my right arm?' I used to think. I had walked up and down the corridor in the hospital in Clontarf, with the aid of a walker and someone by my side. This helped to keep the muscles in my legs moving but it also served to accentuate the reality of my newly acquired disability. So, in effect, I locked myself away in the house, basically only leaving to attend the out-patient clinic in St James's which I did every few weeks.

When the accident happened, I was told that I was looking at eight weeks before my arm would heal. After eight weeks I was told that a "butterfly fracture" of the bone was still visible and, consequently, the bone itself was refusing to knit. This didn't come as any great shock to me, as every time I stood up I could feel the bone moving around in my arm, showing, I thought, no real sign of improvement. The prospect of surgery was mooted again. Whereas when the accident happened I was very keen for them to surgically fix it, now that the fear of possible nerve damage had been implanted in my head, I was scared witless. I had seen the effect, what I hoped would be, a temporary loss of my arm, was having on my quality of life. I knew that if that was to become permanent, then I would rather not live. Again I do not make that statement lightly or in a glib manner. When your life is as crappy as mine had irrefutably become, and has the potential to get even crappier, then I firmly believe that you are entitled to voice your view that your life may just be becoming too horrible to continue with. Undoubtedly it is an unpalatable course to consider someone taking and it leaves psychological debris and carnage in its wake. But instead of taking a high moral view of such a decision, try instead to imagine what living that person's life would be like for a while. If you think about that maelstrom of misery, frustration and unhappiness, can you then say that you do not respect the decision which they have made? It is said that suicide is a permanent solution to a temporary problem. But my incapacity was no longer looking like a temporary problem to me. It had all the makings of being permanent and utterly horrible.

I think that it is fair to say that a good deal of procrastination went on regarding whether or not to perform surgery. I used to be almost physically sick with worry before each out-patient appointment – hoping against hope that my arm would have improved, yet knowing, from the way that it felt, that it just wasn't any better. I sat for so long staring out the front window of my house that I was like a modern day James Stewart starring in my own version of 'Rear Window'. Intense feelings of anger and frustration built up inside me.

At the same time I was determined that I wasn't going to become a TV junkie during this period of isolation. So, maybe it was my way of killing time or probably more likely my way of trying to make sense of my life, but it was then that I started to write this book. Obviously with only one hand functional, thankfully my writing hand, everything was originally written in long-hand. Without any doubt, it kept me from going insane.

There's an old Irish tradition to pray to loved ones who have died, believing that they will always hear your prayers and be looking down on you, taking care of you. But I have to admit that if I heard one more person say, "Don't worry, your Mam will look after you", I would scream. I had had enough of hearing this one day and retorted to one poor unfortunate, well meaning soul: "If that was true then how the hell did she let this happen to me in the first place?"

I started to feel really angry towards Mammy. This anger had started building when I was in hospital in

Clontarf. I felt that she was further from me than she could ever be. If she was in Heaven looking after me, how then was she allowing me to feel so lonely, so afraid of the future and what about the physical pain I was in? This childlike belief that I'd had that she had gone to Heaven and that she would look after me from there was completely blown out of the water. All this served to provide further self-guilt that for the first time I was having negative thoughts towards my mother – and she wasn't even there to bring about such feelings or defend herself against them. And to really put the old tin hat on it, during this time Anne was diagnosed with breast cancer, had to have a mastectomy and potential follow-up treatment. Apart from offering her my ear to bash, I felt completely useless that I wasn't able to support her more. And again I turned this round on Mammy.

I felt that the family had completely lost its way since she died – we were like a ship without a captain, blundering and stumbling from one drama and crisis to another. And yet behind it all, I was really so angry because I knew that no matter who I spoke to about how bad and frustrated I was feeling, and no matter how understanding and supportive they were, they were not Mammy. She would have known what to say. She would have been my rock to cling on to. And I know, without her ever saying it, that Anne felt exactly the same during her huge crisis. Much as I listened to Anne and tried desperately to be there for her, I wasn't Mammy and, in all truth, was a damned poor substitute for her. Someone said at the time of Mammy's death that when the mother of the family dies that the heartbeat of the family stops. And by God was this happening to us.

I went back to the hospital on September 1. When he looked at my latest X-ray the doctors first words were: "I'm nearly tempted to go in and plate the thing once and for all."

Again I expressed the view that that is exactly what I had wanted done from day one, as the fear of a period of inactivity impacting negatively on me was now very much coming true. This together with the fear that I now had regarding surgery, given the doom and gloom predictions of possible nerve damage, was really screwing up my life.

The consultant who had now taken up my care, Mr Smyth, was called in and it was decided to leave my arm in plaster for another five weeks. But I was advised that when I returned I should have a bag packed in readiness for being admitted for surgery.

And so began another five weeks of frustration, boredom, loneliness and a desperately low mood. I felt that it was a futile exercise as I had long given up hope of the arm mending naturally. Friends and family did call regularly and I continued to write the book but I really began to wonder just how much more of this suspended animation I could take. And all the time the thought kept gnawing away at me, that a broken arm to 99.9 per cent of people means a couple of months of inconvenience. To me it was slowly but surely destroying my life.

Somehow I toughed those five weeks out. I turned up for my out-patient appointment with my bag packed. I knew that my arm was still broken as I could still feel considerable bone movement in it. I was seen by a junior doctor who, incredibly, said that she was thinking of having the cast taken off and starting me on intensive physiotherapy. I knew in my heart that she was wrong but I didn't have the courage of my convictions to say so. She said, after some pathetically mild objections from me, that she would leave the arm as it was for another three weeks. She felt that I would, most likely, be ready to start physiotherapy then.

I explained that I had arrived, as instructed, that morning with a packed bag ready for potential surgery.

She laughed, as if I was some sort of eccentric, and said: "Oh no, we're well past the point of surgery now."

In one way I was so relieved, yet I knew that she was wrong – I was certain that my arm was still broken.

I went home to spend what I was positive were three more wasted weeks. I did, however, make calls in the interim to ensure that I was going to be seen by the consultant at my next out-patient appointment at the end of October.

I knew when I saw Mr Smyth's face as I was wheeled into his consulting room on October 27 that the news was not good. He looked at the X-rays that I had had taken that morning and, in a sombre voice, said that he didn't like what he was seeing. The bone was showing no signs of uniting, he didn't know why and that basically surgery appeared now to be the only option. He added the caveat: "There's no guarantee that surgery will be successful."

I asked him what was I to do if surgery was not successful, to which he replied, honestly: "I just don't know. You have to realise that this break was not just an ordinary break, it was a catastrophic one."

He asked me if, as a disabled person, I had never considered that something like this would happen to me which would have such a devastating impact on my life.

I replied: "I hadn't, although when the accident happened I feared that it would start a serious downhill slide in my quality of life and sadly and horrifically that is coming true."

I was in a complete tailspin. My arm was useless as it was and its uselessness was having such a detrimental effect on my life. And yet if I had the surgery, as I surely would now have to, and the operation was not a success, then this temporary blip in my independence would become a permanent feature. I was panic-stricken and didn't know what to do.

Mr Smyth suggested that I go home and think about it. Yet what was there to think about? I could be damned if I did have the operation and I most certainly was damned if I didn't have it. So it was arranged that I go into hospital the following Thursday, November 3, for surgery the next day. Unfortunately, the October Bank Holiday was sandwiched in between. The holiday weekend just seemed to make the days seem endless. This, together with all the fears you could imagine racing through my head, conspired to make the week before the operation, one of the most head-wrecking weeks of my life. Fear, trepidation and terror at being hospitalised again, in a place which held so many bad memories, were the cocktail of horror in my head that week.

I arrived early on that Thursday morning with Dominic. We spent the whole day in the Admissions area waiting for the bed on the ward to be ready. Eventually, at about 4.30 pm, it was. As a result of the inactivity during the day, I couldn't stop my mind from wandering, worrying and fretting about what would happen if the operation did not work out. Unsurprisingly, when the young intern on

Mr Smyth's team, Deirdre, was doing the work up after I was admitted, my blood pressure was something mad like 190/140. Poor Deirdre nearly had a heart attack herself when she saw this and immediately prescribed relaxants to calm me down. I don't really think that they had fully grasped my concerns before this brought it home to them. Okay, a broken arm is a broken arm. It is not a terminal illness. But I couldn't stop imagining where I was going to end up if the operation was not a complete success. I know that by nature I am a worrier but these were seriously major worries and I was struggling to cope with them.

I had a sleeping tablet induced sleep that Thursday night. Still, I awoke around 4 am and, given the way I worry about things that I shouldn't worry about, my first thought was that I needed to get a bowel movement in before the operation. I figured that even if the operation was a thundering success, I might have to be helped to do this, as my arm might be wrapped up even more than it already was. So in I went to the loo whilst the rest of the ward slept. I remember thinking to myself that I really gave new meaning to being "anal" about something, as so much of my time since the accident had been spent fretting and worrying about achieving bowel movements independently.

I was wheeled down to the operating theatre at around 9 am. The relaxants which I had been given were doing their best to work. I was still so worked up that the whole pre-op thing was like some sort of out of body experience – I almost felt as if I was looking down on the whole thing as it unfolded. I was sent off to sleep at around 9.45 am. My fate and the quality of my future life were now very much in Mr Smyth and his team's hands.

I woke up in the early afternoon to a female voice saying: "Wake up Gerard."

For one glorious moment, I thought it was Mammy's voice.

As I slowly surfaced, I became aware of the incredible pain in my arm. It was a pain I had never experienced before, a million times worse than when I had actually broken it. Mr Smyth had advised me that depending upon what they saw when they opened me up, they might have to implant bone from my hip into my arm. He warned me that if this was required then the pain in my hip would be much worse than my arm. I immediately felt for my hip to see if there was any dressing there and was so relieved that there wasn't.

The staff in the recovery room were so good, plying me with copious amounts of morphine until eventually that unreal pain in my arm had all but gone. I was brought back to the ward at around 4 o'clock, the surgery itself having taken close on three hours. I was so comfortable, almost floating, but so afraid to move in case I took myself out of that comfort zone. I remember thinking in my drugged state that for the first time in my life, I was feeling no discomfort, no pain. The feeling of relaxation was so good and I wished that it would last forever.

One of Mr Smyth's team came around soon afterwards to say that the operation, in itself, went as well as they could have hoped. It was now a matter of hoping that the bone would fuse with the metal now implanted in it over the next few weeks.

I was so incredibly relieved that it was over. I was fine except for a horrible sore throat and a subsequent violent cough which I was assured was a consequence of being intubated while under general anaesthetic.

I stayed in hospital for five days.

On the night of the operation itself a young Polish guy had been admitted having broken both his wrists in a building site accident. At about 2 am I noticed a woman standing at my bed, reading my chart. As she had a blue cardigan draped over her shoulders the way they do in TV dramas, I assumed it was the matron!

She said to me: "You had your operation, I see, and it went well."

"Yes," I said.

"Thank God," she replied.

She turned towards the Polish guy's bed. I told her that he was Polish and didn't speak any English. He looked at her rather quizzically and she said, or rather shouted at him: "So you're Polish then?"

She frightened the life out of the poor guy.

'Get me out of this madhouse,' I thought.

Another time during this stay, I was having a bit of a no-sleep night. I went into the toilet at about 3 am and came back after doing the necessaries. I dozed off only too be awoken by about four Gardaí, in luminous yellow jackets, searching the ward. One of the Gardaí, a lady Garda, had a look around my bed. Now I have to admit to being very partial to women in uniform but this was ridiculous!

I never did discover what exactly they were looking for. But if the Garda was searching for the man of her dreams she obviously left disappointed!

On the day I was discharged, my arm was X-rayed – it looked like a little ladder had been implanted into my arm and was now lying against my humerus bone. I was assured that everything was as it should be and was going according to plan.

I was so relieved. For the first time in such a long time I could see light at the end of the tunnel. It had been such a dark and depressing time – such a test for someone who had proven in the past to have had psychological difficulties. And yet I had to admit that I was showing, and had shown, resources of strength in the face of an adversity which would have tested the strongest mind. I had survived some damned dark days – days which I would not have wished on my worst enemy. Foolishly I thought that the battle had virtually been won.

It hadn't.

The demons of yesteryear were mobilising themselves to take one more shot at me.

ELEVEN

FEELING THE SAND
BETWEEN MY TOES

The medical team in the hospital reckoned that it would be at least three months before I could go back to work. My first priority, though, was to be able to drive. It was my one real piece of independence; always has been and hopefully always will be. When that was taken away from me, as had been the case since June 23, then my quality of life became seriously compromised.

At the time of the accident my major fear was that my legs would suffer from the prolonged period of inactivity. When the medics were happy with the state of play with my arm and advised me that it was safe to walk again, my God were my fears confirmed. I have never exactly been nimble on my feet but now I was a man in his early 40s moving with the same pace and ability, as someone twice my age. The muscles in my legs, such as they were, seemed to have died. Simple tasks like filling my car with petrol, going to Church and doing my own shopping, became such monumental physical and, by extension, psychological hurdles to overcome. Worst of all the prospect of going back to work filled me with such stomach-wrenching trepidation. I really felt that in my further weakened state I was an accident waiting to happen.

And yet what was the alternative? I know that many people thought that since my arm was better, what was the problem? But here, in horrible stark terms, was a reminder of the shittiness of having a disability. It takes just one knock to have a domino effect on the rest of you and suddenly your disability becomes so accentuated that at times you wonder if it has just become unmanageable.

I had set myself the target of driving by New Year's Day at the latest. So on January 1, 2006, I struggled to the car. I then strained to get into it, as just about the only one of my four extremities which wasn't weak was my right arm. My initial plan was to drive up and down the road but I was filled with such liberation that I drove out to Clontarf. I pulled in at the side of the hospital grounds and looked at where I had sat or been wheeled around six months previously. While I was now happy to be free to look in at my previous place of incarceration, I also had to be honest with myself. It made me reflect that all the fears I'd had while I was there about my disability moving on at an inexorable pace were now being realised.

I eventually went back to work in late March, but only after five or six weekends of doing dummy runs. There was no way that I was physically ready to go back, but as I had been over six months off work, and was only on half-pay in normal times, the prospect of going on quarter pay was becoming very real. If this happened representations to St Vincent de Paul would then have to be considered! I knew by the way that people in work both looked at me and dealt with me that they saw a different person from the Gerry they'd known pre-June 23, 2005. I now used a walking stick all the time – not just for confidence sake as before, but because I knew that I would have been flat on my arse without it. And agonisingly, my panic attacks made a return visit. Whereas before, I knew how irrational they were, and I was physically able to overcome them, now they were all too rational. I was well aware that physically I was not as good as I had been before the accident and yes, I had to admit it, my disability was getting worse. I spent many days in work, just so terrified and worried about how I was going to get back to my car at the end of the working day. By the time I got home I was psychologically drained. I dreaded meeting anyone in the foyer for fear that they would stop me and talk to me. I knew that if I stopped on the walk to my car I might not be able to mentally, and now physically, move on again. On many occasions I reached my car and realised that if it had been just a couple of steps further away, then chances are that my legs would have given way.

So what was I to do? Use a wheelchair? Considering how embarrassed I was at having to use a stick, the idea that a wheelchair might now be my only choice made me shudder. I'd used one in hospital of course but it was not an unusual sight given the medical setting. When I remembered how reluctant I was using one to get to

secondary school and how thrilled I was to rid myself
of it, I knew that if I started re-using one as an adult, the
chances were the wheelchair would become an adjunct to
me until my last days on this Earth. Whatever mystique I
may have tried to pretend surrounded my disability would
then be well and truly gone. And also I had to consider
that where I worked was hardly wheelchair-friendly.

But what were my other options? To struggle on
waiting for that accident to happen, pride coming before
a fall, only this time literally? Again, negative thoughts
began to fill my head. If I started using a wheelchair,
what would be the next step if it then wasn't enough to
help me cope with my disability? Would I need personal
assistants all the time? Sheltered accommodation? A care
home? Jesus these were fun prospects. And sadly there
were a few times when I fell, thankfully without further
injury, but these falls sapped my confidence. At this stage
it is now virtually running on empty.

In the weeks and months after I started driving again,
I drove to Mammy and Daddy's grave so many times and
begged them to end this torture for me. I asked them to
either restore me to something like I was before, or failing
that to bring me home to them. And, if I am brutally
honest, even after the lapse of time since the accident,
the jury is still out.

* * * *

Two years passed and if I'm completely honest, I seem
to have spent it doing nothing much. I was basically just
dealing with the ordinary every day things of life. The
only difference being that the wheelchair became more

and more a feature in my life. A friend of mine asked me recently how I felt about using the chair. I told her that I hated it but it got me a great view at concerts! I've become a bit of a concert junkie and much as it gives me a great view at concerts, it also means sitting in the designated "Disabled Area". As I have always, and will always, despise my disability, this never appeals to me. Especially on occasions such as the time I brought my niece Ellen to see Westlife and I was the oldest wheelchair user in that section, by a good 30 years!

If I was given three words to describe myself, one of them would unquestionably be "DISABLED". In fact maybe the three words would be "DISABLED, DISABLED, DISABLED". Now I'm sure when friends think of me and if they were asked to describe me, my disability might not feature too highly. Hopefully most of the terms would be favourable. I know I can be a moody sod and that I can be dogmatic, immovable on some opinions. However, I believe that I am basically a good person and am a good friend to have.

And despite the fact that I may paint myself as the greatest exponent of negative thoughts, I try to, and do have, my more positive moments. I know that my negativity towards myself is not shared by those who know and care about me. This was really shown to me recently when Ellen (named after her Nana), was about to make her Confirmation. Anne rang me a few days beforehand to say that Ellen had told her that as part of their preparation, each child had to do a sort of biographical pack, writing a short piece on various topics in their lives. One of the topics was 'The Person I Admire Most in the World'. Some of the other children focused their attention on famous

people. When Anne read me Ellen's piece it absolutely
blew me away:

'The person I admire most in the World is my Uncle
Ger. He has a disability which affects his spine and he has
had this since he was born. A couple of years ago he fell
and broke his arm and needs to use a wheelchair more
and more now. After all he has been through, I think he
has a great attitude to life. If I was half as happy as he is,
then I would consider myself very lucky.'

And I look at my other nephews and niece, who
vicariously I look upon as the children I never had. I
can honestly say that not once have they made me feel
anything other than their uncle, disabled or otherwise.
Two of them are my Godsons, Ciarán and Cathal, and
I'd like to think that they wouldn't swap me for anyone
else. Daryl, who spent the first year of his life living with
us while Liam and Mary house-hunted, is still in my
mind's-eye the baby I used to dote over, even though he
now towers over me. As does young Liam, who, like his
brothers, I failed to indoctrinate into the faith of Chelsea
Football Club! And alas, I think I failed to indoctrinate
Adam into football at all! As for Fionn, I have a feeling
that Croke Park will be graced many times in the future
by that young man. Sadly it will be for his homeland of
Kildare rather than Dublin. And then there's Jenny whose
smile, like Ellen's, should be available on prescription as
an anti-depressant. Those young ladies will break many
hearts in the years to come. Not that I plan on allowing
any boys to pursue them without serious vetting from me
first! God I'm sounding like Mr Chips now!

So why then does my disability feature so prominently
in my description of myself?

It is because throughout my life, every day of it, my disability has been the most tiresome, rotten, debilitating bastard of a noose around my neck. Now I know that there are many disabled people, or whatever politically correct title currently prevails, who claim that they have accepted their disability with a good grace. Some even say that they wouldn't want to change their lives, that they are so comfortable with their disability that they have learned to love it. I find that simply a load of bollocks.

In defending my point of view a little more eloquently let me not generalise but personalise. My disability has stopped me doing so many things. I have tried in broad brush strokes to show how best I coped through childhood with it. But behind it all was the terrible and incredible frustration I had inside me as a child. It is a frustration that a young child is just not emotionally or psychologically equipped to cope with nor, in truth, should be expected to. The times when I longed as a child to be able to dribble past someone with a football; to cycle a bike without babyish stabilisers on them; to climb trees; to walk to school with my friends instead of being pushed there in a wheelchair by my Ma; to bring my dog for a walk on his lead; to take stairs two at a time, instead of clinging onto the banister rail or if there wasn't a rail, by arseing my way down; to not be constantly worrying that my calliper might break and to fear the physical pain and mental solitude I would face while waiting for it to be fixed; to look at girls admiringly, and yes lustfully, while my hormones were racing uncontrollably around my young body and long for them to look back at me in a similar way rather than ignoring me as the disabled young fella.

One of the weirdest longings I have always had is to

be able to walk along a beach and feel the sand between my toes. Even watching people do this on holiday programmes on TV always gets to me. It sounds wacky, I know, but again it is just one of the simple things in life which everyone takes for granted yet which has been and always will be denied to me.

I could go on. And much as my Ma did to make my burden of life lighter, there were just some things which that wonderful woman couldn't do. I know that she was intuitive enough to know that I struggled with all those frustrations, and more, when I was a child.

Then when you leave those childhood experiences behind you, adolescence and adulthood await you. The amount of time that I have spent in my adulthood worrying about going places, not because I was shy or anything like that but because the place might be inaccessible or the calliper might break. Even worse the thought that I might lose my balance and fall over in front of friends or work colleagues, was too horrible to calculate. The times that I have gone on reconnaissance missions to check out places before agreeing to go, have destroyed my soul. When I find that the place is, or more accurately should be, okay, then I might visit it a couple of times more just in case I have missed something on my first reccie. More often I find a place which is going to cause difficulties, such as steps without a rail, steps with a rail but which are too steep, or that real bugbear of mine, places where the ramp leading up to a building is so steep Chris Bonnington would struggle to climb it. This is so true also of footpaths which are supposedly sloped to allow wheelchair users and people pushing buggies to use them more easily. In reality for people like me, whose walking ability is severely limited, these sloped paths are more hazardous than a bloody great step. When I do find places which are so obviously an accident waiting to happen to me, panic sets in and the lexicon of excuses is consulted in order to get myself out of attending. How I wish down the years that I just had had the balls to tell people the real reason. I would have loved to say that I just wouldn't be able to safely and independently get into the building that they were having their party, wedding reception, or the Church that their family's wedding or funeral was in.

How incredible it must be to not have to worry about such things. But when you have a disability you do worry and traumatise yourself over such things, or perhaps more specifically I do. People may say: "There's always someone there who'll help you." But don't they realise that you already feel different to everyone else, asking for their physical help would merely be screaming out the difference even more. And after all, one of the keys to happiness in life is to be able to integrate seamlessly with others, rather than set yourself apart from them.

And, although it would, or rather should, not happen, in these more enlightened times there is always the fear that you would be refused service in places, pubs mainly, because of your disability. It is futile for people to tell me that it beggars belief that this could happen. It has happened to me and it left me, to put it mildly, utterly deflated.

It occurred in one well known pub in Dublin when I was out for a drink one night with a friend. I stood at the bar for ages trying to order our drinks. I watched, as people who came up to the bar after me were served, thinking, innocently, that the barman hadn't noticed me.

When finally I got fed up waiting, I asked the barman why he was ignoring me.

"I'm not serving you," he replied.

"Why not?" I asked, in a mixture of amazement and confusion.

"I don't have to give you a reason," he said.

Thinking that this may be some sort of a wind-up, I said to him: "Well I'd like you to give me a reason."

Dismissively, he said: "Okay, I served you drink here before and you gave it to a minor – now there's your reason."

Given the fact that that was the first time I had been in the establishment and the fact that it's pretty difficult to confuse me with somebody else, the penny suddenly dropped. How embarrassed was I when I got back to the table and told my friend that we had to leave. In fairness to her, she was almost angrier than I was when I told her what had happened.

I wrote a letter of complaint to the manager of that fine establishment which I delivered personally to him the following day. Without even reading it, he tore the letter up in front of my face and threw it at me saying: "I've never refused people like you service."

He seemed very well-informed of the previous evening's events. People like me! Did he mean people like me who had been given this special gift from God? Cheers God, Nice one, Thanks for that.

Nothing similar ever happened but it planted a seed that it could.

I have also encountered some strange people in the medical profession who seem to take something of a novel approach when dealing with disability such as mine. Two consultants, in particular, spring to mind.

The first, who I always found rather gruff in any of my dealings with her, asked me one day if I would mind if she brought some students into the consulting room. This was on my annual visit to see if my disability was degenerating in any way. I always kept these appointments in the vain hope that a radical new experimental procedure had come about which might cure me. Alas!

Anyway I said that I didn't have a problem with the consultant bringing her students in. So I'm there sitting on the treatment table, trousers off, callipers off, waiting for her to examine me. They arrived in, around half a dozen medical students plus the consultant. Without any preamble she said to me: "Okay, get up and walk."

I automatically reached for the callipers, to put them back on.

"No, without them," she said.

I pointed out that she knew that I couldn't walk without the callipers.

"Just try will you," she said.

Again I pointed out that I would fall on my face if I tried.

"Well you'll never know if you don't try," she said in a terse voice.

I felt like saying, and regret now that I didn't: "Listen you stupid bitch, do you not think that as a child in the privacy of my own house that I tried on so many occasions to walk without these things, hoping that some miracle might occur and I could do it."

For that is what I did so many times and so often I couldn't even take one tiny step unaided without falling. And that is exactly what the consultant wanted her students to see, I'm sure.

"Oh very well then, don't," she said in her usual brusque way.

I'm glad, for once, that I had the moral strength to refuse to comply.

The other consultant was a man who was prone to bouts of eccentricity. On one of my visits to him, he came into the consulting room, when again I had no callipers on. He looked at me and said: "Would you ever consider letting me amputate that left leg? Look at it, it's useless."

To illustrate his point, he lifted my left leg up and then let it go. It swung backwards and forwards like a pendulum, unable to stop of its own volition because he was right, it is useless. I stopped it swinging with my hand and asked him what benefit I would get from having the leg amputated. As I have worn a thigh length calliper on my left leg since birth this was a new approach. I knew that my spine was so bad that it has left my left leg virtually worthless and that my right leg basically has to do the work of both legs, but nobody had ever mentioned amputation before

"None really," he said. "You might be better off with an artificial leg, although having your leg amputated at your age might cause you a couple of problems."

As I was in my mid-20s at the time, I know I shouldn't have but I couldn't resist asking: "Like what?"

"Well you could pick up a post-operative infection which might kill you, that's providing you didn't die during the operation or you could end up with "phantom leg syndrome" which might drive you mad," he said.

I politely declined his very generous offer! I could

count on the fingers of one hand, or on the toes of one useless leg, the amount of times that I visited that hospital after that.

I'll never forget my mother's reaction when I got home after these two incidences and told her what had happened. She was a very placid woman, with an even temperament, which she didn't pass on to me. How I calmed her down then though I'll never know!

And then there is the seemingly commonly held view that a disabled person is in some way asexual. Again let me personalise this. I have had lots and lots of difficulties, both physical and psychological, throughout my life. I have never, ever had any problem with feelings of passion and desire coursing through my veins. I love the company of women, always have done and always will do. Some I have viewed as friends, with a boundary line neither crossed nor considered crossing. Some I have been absolutely crazy about and thought that those feelings were reciprocal. One girl in particular rocked my world, floated my boat, you name it I felt it for her. She told me that my feelings were most certainly not one-sided, only to have a sudden and dramatic change of mind when my heart was well and truly hers. I had pinned so many hopes and dreams on that relationship, short as it was, as I was so comfortable with this girl and she seemingly was with me. My disability was there, and we spoke about it openly and how it impacted on my life, yet it seemed like such a minor impediment to the future. I remember feeling so close to this girl and revelling in the incredible buzz that I got, knowing that she was close to me. I wanted to tell her that I loved her because I truly did but I was so afraid to do it in case she ran a mile.

"How could such a gorgeous looking girl with such a caring personality love me?" I kept asking myself. And yet I did pluck up the courage to tell her, although I was fully expecting her to bolt through the nearest exit.

But she didn't. She told me that she loved me and for once I felt whole; I felt valued; I felt like Gerry Maguire the man rather than Gerry Maguire the disabled man.

That is why I was affected so much by her change of heart. I felt almost as if my last chance of love and happiness had gone. And she left me with the thought racing through my head that maybe she had begun to see me as the disabled man and it became too much for her. I wanted to ask her the question but, in truth, was terrified of hearing the answer.

My heart has been battered and bruised by these unrequited and sometimes, what I thought, requited loves. And I know that some of these relationships, or potential relationships, did not run their course due to the spectre of my disability entering into the equation. That is not self-pity, it is self-realisation. For I know that I would find it difficult to begin and ultimately maintain a relationship with a girl who had a disability such as mine. I know the hypocrisy screaming from that statement is deafening but I am just being honest. You see I am not saying that people should view having a disability any differently to how I view it – that it is a king-size pain in the arse.

Some well-intentioned friends have suggested over the years that I should talk to someone professionally about my feelings of resentment, and downright hatred, of my disability. I did it once when my disability introduced irrational panic into my life. But such counselling, or any other form of counselling, can never remove the fact that

I hate my disability.

I hate being disabled and all that being disabled entails.

This is not a recently developed feeling. I have felt it from my earliest recollections as a child and it has grown steadily into adulthood and now into middle age. The additional torments which my disability has caused, such as alcoholism and panic attacks, has only made me despise it even more.

The months after breaking my arm gave me time, too much time maybe, to be able to quantify just how extensively my disability impacts upon my life. As my balance was so compromised, with my arm in plaster, and as I was then so extremely weak post-surgery, I was forced into using a wheelchair. It made me appreciate, though if I'm honest I always did, that my disability could have been so much worse than it was. I have seen many other disabled people much worse off than me who have left me thinking: 'Christ I'd never cope with that.' And yet they do "cope" because they have to.

Or do they?

Sometimes I think that maybe being in a wheelchair all the time would be easier. Certainly I have been able to compare the two and from a socialising point of view, a mobility difficulty is much harder to deal with. Either way, I'm left to ponder whether I should try to struggle on with my decreasing mobility or put my pride in my pocket and accept that walking has too many perils and resign myself to the wheelchair. Cracking choices aren't they!

I believe in God – I am a practicing Catholic, very much a la carte at times, but I do practice. And despite all the slings and arrows which have come and continue to come at me, I believe that I will always practice my religion. But one tenet of Catholicism which I struggle with (and what a tenet to struggle with) is the Church's stance on abortion. Abortion as a form of family planning or latent contraception is wrong – no doubt in my mind about that. Abortion of a pregnancy which is the result of violence or abuse should be utterly and completely the decision of the woman concerned, with appropriate psychological support and guidance. It should never result in the woman being stigmatised for having made the decision either. And then there's my field of excellence – abortion of a pregnancy where tests during those nine months have shown that the child will be born with a serious disability I feel should, if not be encouraged, then at the very least, be explored. This is not me veering towards any form of ethnic cleansing – this is purely and simply the firmly held view of one who has trodden the path of a seriously disabled person's life.

It is so utterly awful for the vast majority of the time – from physical pain and restriction to psychological torment. You can have so many hopes and dreams but pretty quickly you have to minimise them. You realise that while they are easily within the grasp of most others, to you they are an Everest. For example, how many disabled people do you know who are in a loving relationship with children solidifying it? Not many I bet. A more accurate scenario is that the disabled people you know either live by themselves or are in sheltered accommodation, where life ticks by for them. They are existing, rather than actually living, immersed more often than not, in loneliness. If a disabled person lives with elderly parents they will live in fear about what will happen to their son or daughter when they've become incapable of looking after them, through illness or death.

I know that my so dearly loved, late mother would be horrified to hear me voicing aloud my view that there have been many times when I've wished that she hadn't given birth to me. Am I betraying her? Am I now, over 40 years later, agreeing almost with that doctor who advised her to put me in a home and forget about me?

No. I am saying that she deserved a lot more than sacrificing so much of her life for me. She ought to have had so much more time for herself than I, or more specifically my disability, allowed her to have. For that Ma, I am deeply, deeply sorry.

Looking back on that evening when I kissed her goodbye as she lay in her coffin, that is really why I was saying sorry to her. I took up so much of her time and attention and yet I know that if she had her life over again she would do it all again in a heartbeat. But that doesn't make it right.

So what exactly am I saying? I am saying unequivocally that if my mother had been informed that the baby she was carrying would be as disabled as I am; that if she had taken the decision to stop that potential life from turning into a reality then, there is not a single part of me that would have blamed her for having done so.

So if there is a mother now faced with that dilemma, no one, Pope or pauper, should condemn her for choosing to terminate that pregnancy. If she believed it would be too much for her to cope with or that she could not allow a child to have to face a life of certain difficulty upon difficulty, then that is her decision to make.

I do not say such things with false bravado and I do

not believe that what I am saying is in anyway egregious. I would stand before Our Lord himself and voice my opinion. After all, I think that over 46 years of living such torture entitles me to give an opinion. I genuinely do not believe it could be perceived as being wrong to prevent what is certain to be a miserable life from beginning. After all, you wouldn't expect a Cocker Spaniel to have to go through such torment. Why the hell, then, should you expect a human being to?

So is it all doom and gloom? My view on it all hasn't been helped by my being so self-analytical. If I had accepted my disability, settled for my lot, found someone who could love me as I loved them, then maybe, just maybe, I could have hacked it better. And yet maybe the optimist in me says that it's not too late. Maybe that wonderful person who sacrificed so much of her life for me, who spent so much time fighting my corner when she was alive, is still fighting my corner from her heavenly home.

Maybe, just maybe …

FOR MORE GREAT TITLES FROM MERLIN SEE OVERLEAF

Available from all good bookshops

LINES I LOVE

MARY KENNEDY

ISBN: 978 1903582 763
RRP: €12.99 hardback

"Life is mostly froth and bubble,
Two things stand like stone.
Kindness in another's trouble,
Courage in one's own."
Adam Lindsay Gordon

Finding a yellowed copybook when she was clearing out her mother's house, Mary Kennedy was surprised to discover a collection of quotes that her Mam had written down, over the years. Some of them Mary knew; the moralistic ones were especially familiar, as her Mam had quoted them to her children, but others she didn't know. The coincidence is that Mary does the same thing.

In Lines I Love Mary Kennedy combines her mother's pieces with her own collection of sayings and quotes. Built up throughout her life, they all hold some special meaning for her – some are uplifting and motivational; others are of sentimental and nostalgic value. From childhood poems and adult wisdom, to lines about friendship, death, Africa, children and inspirational women, they all have one thing in common – they make her stop and think.

For all those moments when you're looking for the perfect phrase, *Lines I Love* will give you just what you need.

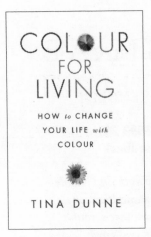

COLOUR FOR LIVING

HOW TO CHANGE YOUR LIVE WITH COLOUR

TINA DUNNE

ISBN: 978 1903582 75X
RRP: €19.99 paperback

What colour do you think of when you hear the words Empowered! Passionate! Sexy!

I bet your answer was red!

Similarly Tranquillity! Calmness! and Serenity! conjure up many shades of blue in our minds. Why do we associate a particular colour with a feeling or emotion and what other impact does colour have on our lives?

In *Colour for Living* Tina Dunne takes you through a spectrum of colour. Find out what colour to wear to put a pep in your step, combat fatigue, de-stress, feel confident and much more. Colour can infiltrate our personalities, which in turn impacts on our daily lives, our careers, ambitions, our choice of friends, lovers, even enemies!

However colour not only has an effect on our emotional well being, it plays a big part in our daily diet and nutrition. Tina looks at the nutrient properties of different coloured foods, what benefits they hold and how much of them to eat. Wonderful healthy and nutritious recipes are listed at the end of each chapter to help promote and maintain a healthy and happy life.

Colour for Living is your beautiful, colourful and vibrant guide to interpreting colour in your life and how we all can benefit physically and emotionally by making the most of the many colours around us.

'Out of this horrendous story of abuse a powerful voice emerges.'
Joe Duffy, rtê

DADDY PLEASE DON'T

BARBARA NAUGHTON

ISBN: 978 1903582 855
RRP: €12.99 paperback

One Sunday morning Barbara's mother told her eight-year-old daughter to tidy up her bedroom. At first Barbara was happy when her father came in to help but what he did next changed her life forever.

In *Daddy, Please Don't* Barbara talks about the six years of physical and sexual violence that she suffered at the hands of her sadistic father, often when the rest of her family were in the house.

She tells of his repeated threats to kill her if she ever told anyone and the two times he actually tried to murder her. The final attack occurred when she was 18 and as he was raping and choking her, Barbara made a vow – if she survived, she would come forward and get some justice against her father.

The shocking details of abuse revealed in the court case in 2002 tore her family apart. As claims of political corruption then emerged, the trial rocked the nation. Through it all Barbara prayed that her nightmare would end and that she would finally find some peace

Daddy, Please Don't is Barbara's story.

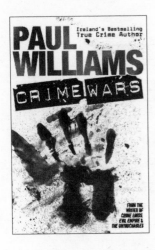

CRIME WARS

PAUL WILLIAMS

ISBN: 978 1903582 831
RRP: €14.99 paperback

Crime Wars is a chilling exposé of Ireland's brutal underworld from the beginning of the new Millennium. In this powerful investigation Williams reveals the stories behind the gangland warfare that erupted, with devastating results, at the start of the 21st Century. He exposes the godfathers and the stories behind the international drug deals, the murders and the mayhem which have all dramatically escalated since the year 2000.

Williams reveals the secret worlds of brutal godfathers Martin 'Marlo' Hyland and paedophile, drug trafficker Christy Griffin. He tells the chilling inside story of the 'cursed' Finglas murder gang and the blood-soaked McCarthy/Dundons in Limerick.

Crime Wars uncovers the background of the horrific Grand Canal double murder – one of the worst atrocities of recent years – and tells the story of Joey the Lip, a desperate young man who became a vital witness in a gruesome execution case. Williams also follows the trail of the Syndicate, a huge international drug trafficking conspiracy organised by Irish criminals, which led to one of Europe's biggest drug seizures.

Crime Wars is a terrifying account of organised crime in modern Ireland.

THE OUTSIDERS

Exposing the Secretive World of Ireland's Travellers

EAMON DILLON

ISBN: 978-1903582-67-1
RRP: €12.99 paperback

The Outsiders uncovers the secretive world of Irish travellers, where prejudice, crime and a burning loyalty to family, clan, and tradition, have made the community ignore external influences.

Eamon Dillon investigates Irish travellers and their worldwide drive to succeed – a hunger that has taken some traveller gangs into the realms of fraud, illegal boxing, home invasions, armed robbery and drug-dealing.

From Bejing to London, Dillon reveals illegal operations by successful Irish travellers, such as the Rathkeale millionaire traveller-traders, the Texan con-artists and the cowboy builders that besiege UK home-owners. These travellers have conquered racism and physical hardship to become modern day pavee princes.

Dillon also exposes another side to life as an Irish traveller, where traveller-on-traveller crime is a major problem and murderous feuds can claim the lives of innocent travellers.

Of an estimated 50,000 Irish travellers worldwide, some will always refuse to bend to the rules of society because they are – the Outsiders.

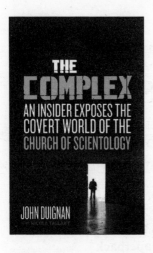

THE COMPLEX

An Insider Exposes the Covert World of the Church of Scientology

JOHN DUIGNAN
with NICOLA TALLANT

ISBN: 978-1903582-84-8
RRP: €12.99 paperback

For the first time ever, a former high-ranking Scientology member is lifting the lid on life inside the world's fastest growing cult. In *The Complex* John Duignan reveals the true story behind the 'religion' that has ensnared a who's who list of celebrities and convinced thousands of ordinary people to join up.

Celebrities like Tom Cruise and John Travolta may give a friendly public face to the cult of Scientology but behind the scenes Duignan reveals how an insatiable money-making, and power hungry, machine is driving the Church ever forward, crushing every critic in its wake. He exposes the fanatical paramilitary group, known as the Sea Org, that lies at the heart of the so-called Church.

In *The Complex* he looks back on the 22 years he served in the Church's secret army – the hours of sleep deprivation, brain-washing and intense 'religious counselling' he endured, as he was moulded into a soldier of the Church. He talks about the Church's military training programme and the punishments meted out to anyone who transgresses, including children.

The beliefs of the Church of Scientology might sound like something from a science-fiction book but *The Complex* reveals that their growing power base is a shocking fact.

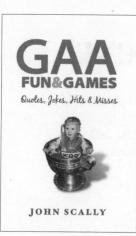

JOHN SCALLY

GAA

FUN AND GAMES

JOHN SCALLY

ISBN: 978 086327 9478
RRP: €9.99 hardback

From hurlers on the ditch to footballers on the pitch, this book is a must for anyone who enjoys our national games. Inspiring as they do such extremes of love and hate, Gaelic games are the ideal breeding ground for memorable quotations and amusing anecdotes.

GAA Fun & Games is laced with laughs, ranging from the warped to the wicked and the shameless to the shocking. A who's who of Gaelic games: everyone who is anyone is here, cutting through the walls of waffle and honouring their wit and side-splitting humour.

Players, managers and pundits are represented as well as some famous names who know little about sport but are always good for a quote. Their words are every bit as entertaining as their achievements, sometimes much more so.

If laughter is the best medicine this is the book your doctor would recommend.

Lost. Grey male cat. Unfriendly. Answers to the name of Pat Spillane. Neutered.

Notice spotted in Castlebar.

Managing a county team means commitment. Of course, so does insanity.

Sean Boylan

FAMINE

LIAM O'FLAHERTY

ISBN: 978 1903582 202
RRP: €12 paperback

Famine is the story of three generations of the Kilmartin family set in the period of the Great Famine of the 1840's. It is a masterly historical novel, rich in language, character and plot, a panoramic story of passion, tragedy and resilience.

'O'Flaherty is the most heroic of Irish novelists, the one who has always tackled big themes, and in one case, in this great novel, succeeded in writing something imperishable ... Mary Kilmartin (the heroine) has been singled out by two generations of critics as one of the great creations of modern literature. And so she is.' *Irish Times*

'The author's skill as a storyteller is at times breathtaking. This is a most rewarding novel.'
Publishers Weekly

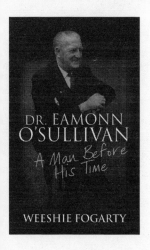

Dr Eamonn O'Sullivan
A Man Before His Time

WEESHIE FOGARTY

ISBN: 978 086327 9430
RRP: €14.99 paperback

In *Dr Eamonn O'Sullivan – A Man Before His Time* Weeshie Fogarty recounts the life and times of an extraordinary Kerryman. As trainer of the Kerry football team, to a momentous eight All-Ireland senior victories in 1924-26-37-46 and again in 1953-55-59-62, including the jubilee win in 1953, Dr Eamonn was a legend in his own time.

For the first time ever, Dr O'Sullivan's autobiographical account, incorporating his innovative training methods, his dealings with the GAA and the building of the Fitzgerald Stadium, his time as Resident Medical Superintendent in the Killarney Mental Hospital, his passionate interest in rehabilitative care and his personal writings, are all reproduced here.

With interviews contributed by GAA greats from past and present, including Kerry trainer Pat O'Shea, Dan Kavanagh, Tom Long, Mick O'Connell, Johnny Culloty, Jerome O'Shea, Sean Murphy and personalities such as Donie Sheehan, Hugh O'Flaherty, Senator Maurice Hayes of Down and Minister John O'Donoghue, the insights into the secret of Kerry football make for fascinating reading. Dr Eamonn's sons also speak candidly about their father, giving an unique insight into the man at home and far away from the maddening crowds.

Weeshie Fogarty's *Dr Eamonn O'Sullivan – A Man Before His Time* is a fitting tribute for the man whose methods changed the art and science of Gaelic football forever.